Praise for **DOC**

MW00582306

. . . .

"Dr. Shapiro has written a compelling book about the events in the immediate aftermath of a major nuclear plant accident in a setting where the government leadership does not want the truth known. Her story is told from her personal perspective as a young physician, with family living in the region, treating patients suffering from radiation injury from the accident but unable to tell them the reality behind their injury or their prognosis. Her personal perspective does not end there, because she went on to immigrate to the US and become a scientist with special expertise in radiation injury. Thus her story is particularly insightful into the actual events surrounding the accident in Chernobyl. This book should be required reading for students from upper grades of elementary school through college—and their parents."

—HAROLD SWARTZ, MD, PHD, MSPH, *The Geisel School of Medicine at Dartmouth Professor of Radiology, Medicine (Radiation Oncology) and The Dartmouth Institute*

"Alla Shapiro's book is a dramatic personal and professional journey woven into the history of her home countries, peppered with humorous anecdotes. A young paediatric haematologist saving lives with limited resources in Kyiv as the Chernobyl disaster unfolds, and discovering how the authorities hide the real extent of the disaster. Mother, daughter and grand-daughter, taking care of her family on their way to safety. Oncologist and medical officer in the top USA government agency working on medications against radiation-induced illnesses she witnessed so closely. One life, two countries, crossroads of two centuries."

—OLGA MARTIN, PHD, *Visiting Professor, University of Bern; Associate Professor, University of Melbourne*

"Alla Shapiro took me along on her odyssey, from the Soviet Union to the streets of Washington, DC, from the Chernobyl nuclear disaster to the COVID-19 pandemic, all the while filling me with emotion and having me "...marvel at the human capacity to resettle and build a better life."

—BORIS LUSHNIAK, MD, MPH, *Dean and Professor, University of Maryland School of Public Health; Rear Admiral (retired), US Public Health Service; Former Deputy US Surgeon General; Former Assistant Commissioner for Counterterrorism Policy, FDA; Son of immigrants from Ukraine*

"Dr. Shapiro's first hand narrative of one of the most disasters in the 20th century is very compelling. Despite Soviet-sponsored obfuscation and misinformation, challenging environmental conditions, and in the midst of religious persecution, she responds with strength, grace and humanity. She turns dark experiences into upfliting stories. Her description of the immigrant experience is very timely given the resurgence of nationalism all over the world. America is lucky to have Dr. Shapiro as one of the world's premier experts in radiation medicine helping shape our national preparedness and response efforts."

—Luciana Borio, MD, *a leading expert on COVID-19 working with the Biden transition team; previously Director for Medical and Biodefense Preparedness at the National Security Council*

"This is a wonderful story of human resilience in the face of tremendous adversity. It is a warm and loving, poignant and upsetting, humorous and exasperating story full of adventures many not welcomed but adventures, nevertheless. For any historian who wants a taste of what Chernobyl was like, read nothing more than the terror and distress parents must have felt asking strangers to take their children on the train out of Kiev. There are so many lessons described herein especially when those in power subvert science and the facts, incite hatred of those who are different all of which leading to increased toll on the population. Dr. Shapiro was a keen eye for details, and these details are able to bring the reader into the situation. In our current world of so much uncertainty this memoir gives strength to the human spirit and brings important lessons to keep in mind as we face potential untold consequences from other disasters to come."

—Nelson Chao, MD, MBA, *Donald D. and Elizabeth G. Cooke Professor; Chief, Division of Hematologic Malignancies and Cellular Therapy/BMT; Director, Global Cancer*

"This ground level, personal account of the Chernobyl catastrophe by a Ukrainian pediatrician is a riveting, fast read...the reader gains a keen understanding of the ethical dilemma of conscripted physicians who were forced to endure, as they worked tirelessly to understand and treat a unique spectrum of radiation-associated injuries that they had never before encountered. The relevance of Dr. Shapiro's story to today's COVID-19 pandemic and to potential future radiation accidents, malicious use of radioactive materials and nuclear war, is highlighted in the last chapters of the book... this is a must read."

—Nicholas Dainiak MD, FACP, *Clinical Professor Department of Therapeutic Radiology, Yale University School of Medicine*

"Dr. Shapiro's firsthand experience caring for victims of the Chernobyl disaster to her distinguished academic and regulatory career in the USA gives her a truly unique perspective on the intersection between public health and politics. These lessons are as timely for us today America as they were in 1986 during the Chernobyl disaster."

    —CHRIS H. TAKIMOTO, MD, PHD, *Senior Vice President, Gilead Sciences*

"Dr. Shapiro chronicles her life in a country that discriminated against women and Jews and yet rises above it to be a hero, a physician, a scientist and a wonderful mother. From the worst nuclear disaster to a pandemic, Dr. Shapiro reveals that governments that were not prepared and lessons were not learned. Her story is emotional, inspiring and thought provoking. It is a must read for everyone."

    —LAURIE E. SOWER, PHD, *Chrysalis BioTherapeutics, Inc.*

"This story is an intimate, first-hand, personal account of Alla Shapiro, MD., Ph.D. as she endures the trials and tribulations caused by the lies, deceptions, and harsh policies of the socialist regime in the USSR before, during, and after the 1986 Chernobyl radiation disaster.... Few would be able to endure the same hardships that Alla experienced along her journey, but her passion and love for medicine and family gave her the strength and persistence. I wonder what she will tackle next?"

    —BERT W. MAIDMENT, PHD, *Radiation Nuclear Countermeasures Program*
       National Institute for Allergy and Infectious Diseases National Institutes of
       Health USA

"*Doctor on Call* tells the story of the Chernobyl nuclear power plant disaster from the eyes of a young Jewish mother who was both a victim of systemic anti-Semitism in a male-dominated autocratic Soviet Republic and a compassionate responder to the medical and emotional needs of so many lives forever changed by the radiation catastrophe. With growing disillusionment for a government whose actions were at odds with her desire to help those in need, Dr. Shapiro details a personal journey of oppression and tragedy whose convoluted destiny is triumph in a new home. History comes alive in this compelling autobiography of one of America's acclaimed experts in treatment of radiation injury and research into radiation countermeasures.

    —L. ANDREW HUFF, MD, MPH; *former Director of the Armed Forces*
       Radiobiology Research Institute

DOCTOR *ON* CALL

DOCTOR *ON* CALL

CHERNOBYL RESPONDER, JEWISH REFUGEE, RADIATION EXPERT

. . . .

ALLA SHAPIRO, MD

[M]

MANDEL VILAR PRESS

This book is typeset in Minion Pro 12/17. The paper used in this book meets the minimum requirements of ANSI/NISO Z39.48-1992 (R1997). ∞

Designed by Sophie Appel

The author has changed some names to protect the privacy of individuals.

Publisher's Cataloging-In-Publication Data
Names: Shapiro, Alla, M.D., Author
Title: Doctor on Call: Chernobyl Responder, Jewish Refugee, Radiation Expert / Alla Shapiro, M.D.
Description: Simsbury, Connecticut. Mandel Vilar Press [2021]
Identifiers: ISBN 978-1942134-732 (pbk.) ISBN 978-1942134-749 (eBook)
Subjects LCSHL Shapiro, Alla-Family / Chernobyl, First Physician Responder / Jewish Refugee /Immigration to the United States / Radiation Expert, Disaster Preparedness, Federal Drug Administration
Classification LCC   R134 S45 2021 E-book

Printed in the United States

21 22 23 24 25 26 27 28 29 / 9 8 7 6 5 4 3 2 1

Mandel Vilar Press
19 Oxford Court, Simsbury, Connecticut 06070
www.mvpublishers.org / www.americasforconservation.org

Dedicated to my family and friends

CONTENTS

PREFACE

I was one of the first physician-responders to the worst nuclear disaster in history: the explosion at the Chernobyl Nuclear Power Station in Ukraine on April 26, 1986. Amid an eerie and pervasive silence, I treated traumatized children and witnessed frightened families and civilians running barefoot across radioactive sand, carrying stretchers to save others. The images of these victims and of widespread destruction remain in my memory.

A pediatrician and hematologist in Kiev at the time of the Chernobyl explosion, I was dispatched to the emerging nuclear nightmare. Some first responders extinguished fires and cleaned up radioactive debris. We physicians triaged and administered first aid. None of us were given protective clothing or detailed instructions. At international conferences, I am repeatedly asked this question: "What were medical first responders least prepared for at Chernobyl?" My answer never changes: "Everything."

The first part of *Doctor on Call* describes my experiences while responding to the disaster. Some previously published narratives emphasize the Soviets' lack of preparedness for coping with radiation events. My chronicle goes on to recount the lies and deliberate misinformation perpetrated by the government from the outset of the disaster. We first-responder physicians not only worked "in the dark," but, contrary to our principles, we were ordered to participate in the deception of the public.

The bureaucratic lies and cover-ups in the aftermath of the explosion were the final reason my family and I fled the Soviet Union, along with hundreds of thousands of other people. Many of them, like us, had also endured decades of open hostility toward Jews. The Soviet government declared us all stateless, and many were branded as traitors. Each of us defectors was allowed to take, at a maximum, forty pounds of possessions and ninety dollars in cash. Our emotional and historical baggage would be impossible to put down, leave behind, or unpack.

The second part of this memoir describes our emigration experience and our adjustment to living in the United States. Four generations of my family and a diverse group of fellow refugees traveled to Austria and then on to Italy, where my family remained in limbo for six months. We belonged nowhere. Nobody knew if we would ever arrive in the United States, with its promise of freedom and new beginnings.

In the third part, I discuss my professional work in the US, where I became an international expert in the development of medical countermeasures against radiation exposure. At the US Food and Drug Administration, Center for Drug Development and Research, I held the position of medical officer, Counter-Terrorism and Emergency Coordination Staff.[1] With a passion born of heartbreaking experiences, I applied what I had learned from the Chernobyl disaster to my work.

I have tried to follow in the steps of the immigrants who built America over three hundred years. The stories of their resilience, courage, and contributions to society give me hope that, despite any disasters that could destroy us, new days will continue to dawn.

ACKNOWLEDGMENTS

I n the late 1980s, hundreds of thousands of Soviet Jewish refugees made their way from the Soviet Union through Europe to the United States. I was one of them.

Although it was a diverse group, we shared common experiences. We faced "the great unknown" as we entered a different political and cultural environment. For each family, including mine, immigration offered a mixed bag of prospects: some were exciting and others hovered over us like a dark cloud. Our stories of hardships, losses, victories, hopes, and dreams should not be forgotten.

I am indebted to my family, who shared this incredible journey with me. During the most difficult times of being stateless, we tried to support each other. Sometimes we failed, proving that our existence is a mixture of mistakes and missteps. Disappointments and regrets are enlarged in the aftermath of unmitigated trauma.

Fellow refugees have my gratitude for permitting me to chronicle their struggles and perpetuate their legacies of loss and triumphs.

I feel immense gratitude to my chief editor, Glynnis Mileikowsky, for always standing by me and making *Doctor on Call* a reality. Glynnis's professional skills and creativity were essential to this project. Her friendship, expertise, and suggestions helped diminish my weaknesses in this uncharted field of writing.

Many thanks to Victoria Churchville for listening to my stories, re-reading my work, and assisting me with revisions. She helped my voice to emerge from this journey of devastation, immigration, and renewal.

I wouldn't be who I am without my mother, Neli Melman, who has always encouraged and believed in me. Her love is truly unconditional. Thank you for leading me and letting me find my way at the same time. Thank you for seeding the best of you in me.

My dear, beloved daughter, Olga, is my pride, joy, and constant support—my greatest gift. She went above and beyond to help move my project forward. I continue to learn from her how to confront and survive the whirlwind of existence.

I am forever grateful to Olga, her husband, Pasha, and their four adorable boys. Their growing family tree gives me faith in the continuity of life.

My deepest appreciation goes to William Mapes, my husband and best friend, for his critical, and critically important, recommendations. Bill's great patience and enthusiastic encouragement guided and inspired me from the first page to the last.

I am grateful to the team of my colleagues led by Vladimir Bebeshko in Kiev, Ukraine, for the chance to work with them for over a decade. Even in those dreaded Chernobyl days they were not only colleagues at work, but kind and supportive friends.

Special thanks to all my friends, who have carried me through many crises. Irene and Larry Feldman, Alla and Michael Taller, Yulia Spivak and Roman Svirsky, Olga and Eugene Ryzhikov, Irina and Viktor Kopit, Veronika and Vladimir Litvak, Lena and Yuriy Benikov, Tatyana and Leonid Felikson, and Slava and Leon Leykin sustained me in my darkest moments and times of self-doubt. They listened to my endless monologues and to some serious and sometimes odd ideas that I pursued. There will always be a huge place in my heart for them all.

My special thanks go to the amazing and reassuring friends I have made in the United States. I owe profound gratitude to all the Americans who assisted us in navigating the perils on our path: Maria and Kenneth Gibala, Judith and Warren Greenberg, Sue and Martin Levin, Debbi and Peter Friedman, Paul Pevsner, Merry and David Eisenstadt, Benjamin Bornstein and Ellen Sidransky, Jody and Evan Krame, Tania Heller and Sam Messeca, Rick and Mara Williams, Tony and Sheelagh Crowley, Yaron and Delphine Gamburg, Liz Mapes, and Glynnis and Ron Mileikowsky. I have appreciated their kindness, enthusiasm, encouragement, and insight from the day we met, and I look forward to continuing my journey with them.

My loyal friends and dedicated work colleagues deserve to be mentioned: Susan McDermott, Andrea Powell, Karen Smith, Joan Flaherty, Viktor Meineke, Norman Coleman, Brian Moyer, and Richard Hatchett. Our hours of working together were filled with support, their extensive knowledge, laughs, and jokes.

I greatly appreciate everything that Dena Mandel, editor in chief at Mandel Vilar Press (MVP) did for me. Her generosity, patience, and assistance and her faith in me kept me moving toward my goal. Dena spent long hours reviewing more than one draft of my book. Her literary talent added special dimensions to my writing.

I had the privilege of working with Mary Beth Hinton, an exceptional, knowledgeable, broad thinking, and courteous editor. I am so thankful for her treating me as a colleague rather than a struggling first-time author.

I am immensely grateful to Barbara Werden, a talented designer and production manager. Thanks to her professional skills, each picture in this book shines a light on the stories that made their way from the past to the present.

My deep appreciation goes to Sophie Appel, the book designer.

Her imagination and creativity made an impactful cover that did justice to the stories inside.

Finally, Robert Mandel, co-founder and publisher of MVP, deserves lots of credit for being the "key" that opened the door for me into a new world of expression. Robert introduced me to Franz Kafka's statement that "a book must be the axe of the frozen sea within us." Many thanks to him for giving me the opportunity and inspiration to embrace this concept.

DOCTOR *ON* CALL

PROLOGUE

I t is eight o'clock in the morning. For me, this day is different from others. I stare at the clock on top of my refrigerator. I have always admired the design of this clock. Its face is superimposed on an image of a metal cup resting on a saucer. "Steam," in the form of a metallic curl, rises from the cup. I want to freeze the relentless flow of time, measured so precisely in ticktocks. But time never stops because it has no beginning and no end. Today I am scheduled to start chemotherapy, and I expect a drastic change in my life.

It seemed that 2011 would be a favorable year for me. Just a few weeks ago I returned from Poland, having attended the 14th International Congress on Radiation Research, titled "Science as a Public Duty: Following the Ideas and Work of Maria Sklodowska-Curie." The world's scientific community was celebrating the one hundredth anniversary of Madam Curie's Nobel Prize in Chemistry. As a keynote speaker, I delivered a presentation on behalf of the United States Food and Drug Administration (FDA).

I was a hematologist before the Chernobyl accident. After settling in the US, I became, in addition, a pediatric oncologist and an expert on the health effects of radiation. At the conference's dual locations in Warsaw and Krakow, my colleagues presented scientific data about the acute and delayed effects of radiation exposure.

While in Poland I noticed some changes in my health, and I realized that something was wrong. As a physician, it was hard for me to assess my own symptoms the way I would assess the same symptoms in a patient. "This can't be me," said my internal voice. But the results of medical tests revealed that I had colon cancer, one of the most common delayed effects of radiation exposure. My life was shattered into many pieces, like a jigsaw puzzle that I would never be able to put back together.

On this morning, having recently recovered from extensive surgery, I am getting my first chemotherapy treatment. The weather outside is warm, but I am feeling chilled, and the radioactive winds of Chernobyl are blowing through my mind. My husband drives me to the clinic in silent support. Along with some personal belongings, I have brought to the treatment facility not one, but two computers. One is the property of the FDA—I did not want to miss anything going on in my workplace. The other is my personal laptop.

The head nurse greets me and asks, "Doctor, do you remember why you are here?"

This unexpected question reassures me, and I again feel connected to past events, the present world, and to all the victims of radiation that I will continue to care for.

I open my laptop and begin to write this book.

PART I

Chernobyl
Doctor on Call

CHAPTER 1

Nuclear Spring, 1986

I first heard of Chernobyl when my father, Yefim, called me early on the morning of April 26, 1986. A nuclear reactor had exploded near Chernobyl, a city located sixty miles from Kiev. The site was in the small town of Pripyat, just nine miles from Chernobyl. Voice of America (VOA) had broadcast into Ukraine reports of increased radiation levels detected in Sweden. It was first suspected that the radioactive substances released into the air came from one of the neighboring countries.

My dad for many years had gotten the real news about what was going on in the Soviet Union from the VOA and the BBC. He heard the first report, which did not yet mention a nuclear blast, at about 2:00 a.m., the only time he could receive unjammed broadcasts. The world was still unaware that parts of the reactor core had exploded like rockets through the atmosphere. Radioactive fission products of uranium, such as iodine, cesium, and strontium, were catapulted into the atmosphere and spread across vast parts of Europe and the northern hemisphere. When my dad told me about the explosion, I wasn't very concerned. Chernobyl was a little known, nondescript place.

For years I had followed Soviet news reports on US testing of nuclear weapons in Nevada. Yet I was completely unaware of this nuclear power plant so close to home that would soon propel my life and my career into a whole new sphere.

Back on that sunny day of April 26, people went about their daily lives. They were enjoying an unexpectedly warm Saturday morning. In the area surrounding Chernobyl, families mingled outdoors. Many of them headed to the woods to pick the spring's first wild strawberries and mushrooms.

After the explosion, the Soviet and Ukrainian governments issued no warnings and repeatedly insisted over public broadcasts that life should continue normally in the shadow of the disaster. The pervasive official response was to deny and to mislead the public. This approach was embraced by those in the highest positions as well as by the lowliest bureaucrats.

On April 29, three days after the disaster, a friend of my dad called to share some unprecedented events that he had witnessed. His friend Vladimir, a retired airplane pilot who still worked at a large airport in Kiev, noticed something disturbing during the night shift: airport workers had been ordered to manage a frantic scramble for flights out of the city, even as the government news media repeated that the nuclear explosion near the city of over two million people posed no threat. The passengers on these night flights, Vladimir said, were "special and distinguished." They were Communist Party leaders and their families.

For days, Soviet officials were mute about the accident and its rapid deterioration into a catastrophe. Yet while local Communist Party bosses evacuated their own families, hundreds of thousands of ordinary people and their children were encouraged to attend a May

Day parade in Kiev, where radiation had soared above safe levels.[2] On the following Monday, April 28, and in the weeks after the Chernobyl tragedy, life at Children's Hospital, one of the largest hospitals in Kiev, changed dramatically for the medical personnel in the Pediatric Hematology Unit. We were all on high alert, but it was a vague alert. The words "high" and "vague" seem incongruous, yet this is the most fitting way to portray the chaos of the days and weeks that followed the night of April 26, 1986.

I shared a medium-sized office with six other pediatricians. Our boss was the chief of the Pediatric Hematology Unit and also a research professor. Whenever he heard rumors pertaining to Chernobyl and the surrounding areas, he rushed into our room from his private office. One day the professor, as we called him, barged into our cramped room, slammed the door, and stared for a moment, not knowing where to begin. His face was red, and his eyes scanned each corner of the room, as if looking for a hiding space.

"I just got a call that hundreds of children have been evacuated from the thirty-kilometer zone around Pripyat, where Unit No. 4 of the nuclear reactor exploded, and are coming to our hospital."

"Could you please provide some instructions on what we are supposed to do when the children arrive?" I asked him.

"We do not have any instructions or guidance," he replied. "Just exercise common sense. Thousands more children from the surrounding, highly contaminated, areas are already waiting in long lines for us to admit them," the professor added.

For a few minutes, we remained stunned as we tried to absorb the news. During this silence, the telephone rang. I was the closest to it, and therefore the first to hear the "request" that followed. It was non-negotiable, since it came from the top. I immediately recognized our director's voice and was gripped by anxiety and fear. I covered the microphone of the receiver and whispered into the air, "It's Nick." He was the director of the National Institute of Hematology and Blood Diseases, and our hematology unit came under his umbrella. The silence grew heavier as a wave of panic spread through the room.

"Who is responsible for covering hematology cases in Ukraine this month?" the director asked me.

"It's my turn," I responded. *Why was he calling us?* Usually it was a clerk who asked this question and then directed one of us to a place where our medical expertise was needed the most.

"Listen," the director continued. "In one hour, an ambulance will pick you up from work and take you to a place not too far from here."

"Of course," I replied. "Just one question. Should I let my family know that I won't be coming home tonight?"

"I don't know," he answered. "You must decide on the spot." He hung up.

My colleagues remained silent as they processed the brief one-sided conversation they had overheard. Nobody asked me anything. Everyone chose to assume that the director was giving me one of our regular assignments: going as a pediatric hematologist consultant to areas of Ukraine to help solve tough diagnostic cases, or to offer treatment options when other therapeutic approaches had failed.

After a few minutes of silence, Natasha, one of the doctors who was listening to my conversation with the director, took me aside. "Do you really want to go there?" she asked.

I decided that answering her question with another question would be less rude than saying no. So, I posed my question: "Do I have a choice?"

Natasha looked away from me and said, "Well, I think that you do." She went on, "This morning I had a fight with my husband and I don't want to go home and face him tonight, so I could go for you today instead. When it is my turn to do the out-of-town consult, you can switch with me."

This sounded like a very decent proposal, and I agreed without hesitation, as I had already planned something for that evening.

It was a hot spring day. Under her white robe Natasha was dressed in a short-sleeve blue blouse, skirt, and sandals. Her pretty blue eyes looked gray; they reflected sadness and emotional pain. Her golden hair was hanging down her back. One hour later the ambulance arrived. Natasha waved to us and left. The rest of the medical staff stayed at the hospital awaiting the arrival of busloads of evacuees from Pripyat and villages surrounding Chernobyl.

Earlier that day, thirty-six hours after the explosion, the population of Pripyat had received a false "assurance" from the calm voice of a female announcer: "Attention! Attention! In connection with the accident at the Chernobyl atomic power station, unfavorable radiation conditions are developing in the city of Pripyat. To ensure complete safety for residents, children first and foremost, it has become necessary to carry out a temporary evacuation of the city's residents to nearby settlements of Kiev *oblast* [province].

"For that purpose, buses will be provided to every residence today, April 27, beginning at 14:00 hours, under the supervision of police officers and representatives of the city executive committee. It is recommended that people take documents, necessary items, and food products to meet immediate needs. Comrades, on leaving your dwellings, please do not forget to close the windows, switch off electrical and gas appliances, and turn off water taps. Please remain calm, organized, and orderly."

Over 1,000 buses went from Kiev to Pripyat, people boarded them, and the exodus began. Some of the buses arrived in Pripyat in the early afternoon as expected. However, some did not arrive until late at night. Families with children waited outdoors for many hours. As the day died out and the darkness fell, the last buses finally arrived and carried the exhausted people away from the thirty-kilometer exclusion zone.

For some of them it was too late. Two years after that I treated a four-year-old girl with acute leukemia. Her mother told me their evacuation story. She and her daughter—the girl was two years old then—were waiting in Pripyat for the buses when evacuation was announced. Her baby, along with other children, had played in the radioactive sand under the shower of nuclear fallout, breathing the air filled with dense radioactive particles.

The evacuees had packed only the essentials; they were prepared to be away for three days only. Among other betrayals, the Soviet government preferred to keep up the pretense of a "temporary evacuation."

In our unit at the hospital, the next three days seemed endless. As more buses with evacuees arrived at Kiev, scared passengers from Pripyat and surrounding villages were unloaded at different times, and the empty vehicles were moved to the center of the city.

Bus drivers rushed to the public baths to shower. They dropped their radiation contaminated clothes on the floor, chairs, and shelves of the public bath. The emptied buses were blocking one of the main streets, right where my family lived. Teams of workers washed the buses with hoses. Muddy water poured off the buses and streamed down the street, forming large and deep ponds in the populated areas of Kiev. Toddlers and older children splashed in the contaminated water.

Hundreds of families who were evacuated from the thirty-kilometer exclusion zone around Pripyat arrived at the hospital. In the absence of instructions or medical guidance, each of us did the best we could. No one complained that the doctors did not spend enough time with each patient. Time itself became meaningless.

For three straight days and three nights, my colleagues and I didn't leave the hospital. We lived and worked on the pediatric floor. Our family members brought us food and clean clothes. The few existing hospital showers were filled with the incoming children and adults. For most of them, home had become a place of no return. Evacuees also crowded into the hospital registration area. Doctors and nurses waited to gather the medical history on each child and to perform a physical exam. No one cried. No one talked. There was a pervasive sound of coughing among the incoming patients. This red flag put all the medical staff on high alert.

None of us could diagnose the cause of the cough; therefore, no one knew the proper treatment. It became a high priority for us to crack the "cough code." The "happiest" moments occurred when one of us identified a child whose cough was accompanied by fever or shortness of breath. In such cases, the proud doctor placed an order for drugs to treat fever and bronchial spasm.

Unexpectedly, one of the pediatricians from our group blurted out, "Guys! The kids and their family members are coughing because they have inhaled radioactive particles! Who knows what should be done?"

There was a long moment of silence. No one knew what to do. Since the answer was not to be found in any of our medical books, we were forced to innovate. We improvised treatment, using whatever materials were readily available.

One colleague took the initiative and tensely directed, "Go and grab a blanket." I immediately obeyed. While observing my actions, my colleague snatched the belts from a few white robes. Then we placed as many kids as possible on the beds to allow them to be under the blanket "tent."

"Get an oxygen tank!" he commanded. His voice gained strength and confidence. We brought in a few oxygen tanks, turned them on, and the treatment commenced. The oxygen helped to reduce coughing in most of our patients. The kids did not even cry or whine because, if they did, the caregiver would remove them from the tent—not a desirable outcome. Although we never claimed ownership of this invention, it did fit some eighteenth- or perhaps nineteenth-century standards of care.

Another intuitive move was to talk to the children about something funny and calming. Many of them were in shock, most were anxious, and some were clearly depressed. We did what we could to lift their spirits.

Days after the disaster, the medical community remained unprepared. We all desperately needed whatever relevant information could be found. The head of pediatric hematology at the hospital where I worked asked me to stop by the National Medical Library in Kiev to pick up books about the human health effects of radiation exposure. This premier library had the best current sources of medical literature in Ukraine.

I set off in search of information for a presentation that my boss wanted me to make the following day to health care providers. As I walked into the library, I stared in disbelief at rows of empty shelves and display windows. A librarian explained that the library staff had followed an order from "above" to pull from the shelves all the books and scientific journals that contained the word "radiation."

This was the Soviet government's default position: no information means no panic. As a result, the population of Kiev and its vicinity learned about protection from radiation through rumors, which spread rapidly. Many people, including my family, started thinking of evacuating their children. We wanted to send our three-year-old Olga to a "clean" area, but I didn't know where such a place might be.

Very soon after the explosion some scientists managed to gain access to the true numbers reflecting the degree and scope of radioactive contamination. They put together a color-coded map showing the levels of radiation in each area. The colors ranged from angry red to soothing green. One of the neighbors in our apartment building in Kiev was a scientist with a PhD who worked at the Institute of Physics in Kiev. His affiliation enabled him to "smuggle" from his workplace a copy of the map. We finally had a chance to see where the hottest radiation spots were in Ukraine, Belarus, and western Russia.

A few close friends gathered at our apartment. Having grown up in the Soviet Union, everyone feared that authorities would follow them, listen to their conversations, or even put them in jail. We closed the drapes on the windows and unplugged our landline phone. From watching spy movies, we thought that these precautions would spare us from the KGB (Committee for State Security) agents whose job was to catch people who showed too much interest in uncovering the truth. We stood at the table and pored over the smuggled map—and realized instantly that the city of Kiev was in a hotspot.

Alarmed by this news, I borrowed a Geiger counter—a device for measuring radioactivity—from a friend. During the ten-day information blackout, I could check levels of radiation at home, on furniture, on Olga's toys, and on potted plants on the balcony. Two hours later, after crawling from room to room with the Geiger counter, I forbade my daughter to play with her toys.

I felt emotionally numb, my way of protecting my conscious mind from the distress and shock of detecting significant radiation in the safest place on earth: our family home. Yet I was forced to accept the direness of our predicament. Full of fear, I focused on one of Olga's favorite stuffed toy animals, which she was gently hugging and kissing. I slowly moved the Geiger counter along the fuzzy body. The negative results thrilled both of us, and Olga pulled the toy from my hands and kissed it on the nose.

"Wait!" I shouted, "Let me check the nose too!" The next moment we heard the dreaded click, click, click. The radiation level found on the tip of the nose far exceeded the safe limit to which a child could be exposed in an entire year. I buried the toy in the trash, along with some sofa pillows and flowerpots from the balcony.

Common sense prevailed. I couldn't totally rid the apartment of radiation. My family would end up sleeping on the floor without pillows or blankets, eating without dishes or silverware. I realized that we could not live that way. I returned household objects to where they belonged and announced, "Business as usual," with a bravado I did not feel. I cuddled the inconsolable Olga, who hugged a pillow in lieu of her toy. Business as usual became part of everyday life for the people of Kiev and surrounding areas. The winds of life are sometimes unpredictable and rough. I just tried to adjust my sails.

A few days after the explosion, I was called in to a Kiev clinic to consult on a pediatric hematology case. I was to see a sick child and meet with the radiologist to discuss the patient's X-ray results. I had never been to this clinic before and so asked an employee, "Where is your radiology department?"

"Everywhere," he replied nervously, with a wry attempt at humor.

I wasn't upset by this answer. I shared his perception of danger as I prepared to battle this great enemy, invisible and in many other ways undetectable. In the face of the worst nuclear disaster the world had known, nothing appeared "as usual."

Some physicians refused to see patients who came to a clinic or emergency room with diseases or conditions unrelated to exposure to radiation. Their standard response was, "What's the point of treating you, if we are all going to die tomorrow?"

Many of my colleagues and I traveled to the most radioactive areas of Ukraine without protective clothing or any specific instructions. Physicians and so-called "liquidators," teams of civilian and military personnel, entered these areas to triage and help with the cleanup after the radioactive fallout of the explosion.

Between my deployments to contaminated areas, I continued to work at Children's Hospital in Kiev. Medical personnel there evaluated and treated hundreds of children of different ages who were evacuated from Pripyat. As is the standard practice everywhere, each patient's chart was enclosed in a hard "jacket" (cover). Diagnoses were always written on the cover.

Patients who came from Pripyat and surrounding areas were treated for a range of different diseases. However, for most of them the diagnosis was acute radiation sickness (ARS). Several weeks after the explosion, the staff were told that a high-level commission from the Ukrainian Ministry of Health would be visiting their hospital.

The order from above was straightforward: rip off the covers of all charts showing a diagnosis of ARS. Put a new jacket on the corresponding chart along with a new "benign" diagnosis. In this case creativity was not allowed. We were ordered to change the diagnosis to vegetative vascular dystonia. People with this condition of the autonomic nervous system have symptoms of weakness, sleepiness, and depressed mood. Nobody dared to question or argue.

Like many of my colleagues, I felt betrayed. Why should the doctors remain silent after the "father of glasnost," Gorbachev, had preached openness in his nation's affairs? How could revealing the truth be a deadlier killer than actual radiation? Why was there such a need to conceal the Soviet Union's biggest failure?

I asked myself this repeatedly. Answers never came.

CHAPTER 2

Rx For Radiation

Take as (Not) Directed

T he people who lived in the contaminated areas of Ukraine and Belarus had many questions: "Should we give potassium iodide (KI) to our children? Should adults take this medicine too? If so, what is the optimal dose, frequency, and timing of KI administration in relation to the radiation exposure?"

As a physician I was bombarded with such questions. My answer was short and it never changed for the next few years: "I do not know." I noticed that nobody asked me about potential side effects of KI, and I did not ask this question either. I found out about the possible reactions to KI the hard way.

Weeks after the event, we learned that the Chernobyl explosion resulted in the release of substantial amounts of radioactive materials. One of the most prevalent elements was radioactive iodine, which affects the thyroid gland. The result of this exposure is a dramatic increase in thyroid cancer. Other radioactive materials included cesium, plutonium, and strontium radioisotopes. Each of these elements could cause other cancers and leukemia.

People can be affected rapidly by radiation after breathing contaminated air or consuming contaminated milk and leafy vegetables. After entering the body, iodine becomes concentrated in the thyroid gland. Without protection for that gland, those exposed will be at a very high risk of developing thyroid cancer. If given before or in the first six to eight hours after exposure, potassium iodide (KI) will protect the thyroid gland from absorbing radiation, thus significantly decreasing the risk of thyroid cancer. However, this information was not communicated to the medical first responders or the public. Instead, they learned about KI through rumors.

Several days after the disaster, potassium iodide appeared on the shelves of the pharmacies. Horrified parents, including myself, were buying it to give to their children.

One day I was called to the emergency room of the hospital where I worked. Ambulances were bringing children suffering from gastric bleeding. Their parents, lacking knowledge of proper dosing and frequency, had given their kids too much KI. The parents were also unaware that their efforts were too late: the children had been exposed to radiation ten days ago.

Years later while in the US, I learned another "truth" about KI that had been hidden from the Soviet people. A former pediatric endocrinologist colleague of mine told me that protocols for KI administration in case of a radiation emergency had been in place but were not provided to physicians.

In the first few days after this catastrophic event, I understood that the level of radioactive iodine in Kiev, where we lived, was very high. Like many other people, I experienced a nasty metallic taste in my mouth, which I later learned is termed "metal mouth." The physicians and other first responders didn't know that metal mouth is a common symptom after radiation treatment and radioactive contamination of all kinds. I also felt a strong burning sensation in my ears and nose. At the time I couldn't explain these symptoms.

While working in the United States for the Food and Drug Administration, Counter-Terrorism and Emergency Coordination Staff, I learned that the American public has available a vast amount of information and guidance on KI as part of emergency response planning to protect against the effects of radioactive iodine. Details on all the possible side effects of this drug are provided as well.[3]

CHAPTER 3

Olga Leaves and Natasha Returns

A fter it became obvious that we could not protect our daughter from the high levels of radiation noticeable in Kiev, my husband and I decided that it was time to send Olga to one of the unaffected areas of Ukraine. We chose the city of Kharkov because the massive radioactive plume had not reached that city, which was in the "green" area on the map. In addition, Lady Luck was smiling—Olga's aunt Bronya, who lived in Kharkov, invited our daughter to stay with her indefinitely. However, we could find neither an airplane nor a train to take her there. Tickets for the following weeks were sold out everywhere, including on black markets.

Three-year-old Olga stayed at home with her great-grandmother, Berta, under my strict instructions to stay away from the windows. I used bottled water to cook food, and for five days continued hunting for any ticket to the evacuation area. Finally, I was able to buy three tickets to Kharkov, located five hundred kilometers (a little over three hundred miles) from Kiev. Olga was to go there with her two grandmothers.

However, the plan partially failed, and it was my fault. Two days before Olga's departure, I decided to give her liquid potassium iodide

(KI). I filled the dropper with the medicine, but because of its dark color and unpleasant smell, I changed my mind. I quickly emptied the liquid into a glass cup, and placed it on top of a glass cabinet out of Olga's reach. Then I left the room, battling the guilt of not protecting my daughter the way I should.

Alas, my behavior piqued the curiosity of three-year-old Olga, who stepped on the arm of the couch and reached for the medicine. Based on her "past medical experiences" playing with dolls, my daughter thought that a dropper goes into a nose. She started sticking it into both her nostrils. The result was that Olga developed an allergic reaction to KI. Even the residue of the medicine left on the inside of the dropper caused multiple symptoms, such as sneezing, coughing, and sore throat. Her eyes were itchy and watery.

She cried and begged me to go with her on the overnight train the following evening and to leave one of the grandmothers in Kiev for the time being. The next morning, I shared my distress with my colleagues, who seemed sympathetic—except for my boss. I went to his office and asked, "May I take half a day off to go with Olga? This trip is almost eight hours on a train. She is sick, I am concerned that she could get worse, and I would like to be with her."

"No, you have to stay; we need you here. If you go, don't come back."

I pretended that I was prepared for this answer. I would have to say good-bye to Olga at the train station.

Our apartment building was located about ten minutes by car or fifteen minutes by bus from the train station. By the day of Olga's departure, the people of Kiev had succumbed to panic. Everyone was trying to move their children out of the city. However, many people either did not have families or friends who lived in the "clean" areas or could not get tickets to the intended destinations.

The roads that led to the main train station in Kiev were packed. Buses and cars sat bumper to bumper and were not moving. My uncle Joseph, who came to our apartment to say good-bye to his beloved niece Olga, made a suggestion: "Let's walk to the train station; otherwise you will miss the train!" He lifted Olga, placed her on his shoulders, and set out for the train station. The rest of the family walked behind carrying suitcases and Olga's toys.

My mom and my mother-in-law, who escorted Olga to the "clean" city, recollected their experiences of evacuation during World War II. Talking about the present and future seemed to scare them, so they found some comfort in discussing similar episodes from the past.

At that time, evacuation routes led to victory. Many industrial plants of military importance were moved to areas such as the Urals, Siberia, and Central Asia. My grandfather Yakov worked as the chief engineer at a glass factory in Kiev. In 1941 the factory was relocated to Turkmenistan. My mother, her younger brother, my grandmother, and my great-grandmother followed him. All of this occurred before the German conquest of Kiev. If they had stayed in that city, they most likely would have perished in the Nazi massacre at Babi Yar. My family returned to Kiev in March 1945, toward the end of the war.

Moments in history often replicate themselves. On that day in May 1986, we were trying to protect our children from something as dire as war—a nuclear catastrophe. The train was waiting on the platform, and we moved to the ticketed seat numbers. There had always been a strict ticket check prior to every train's departure, but on that day all the prior-to-departure rules were ignored, and access to the wagons was uncontrolled.

Parents who had not been able to buy a ticket put their kids in the hands of strangers, sometimes passing them through open windows and begging passengers to take them to a secure place. Doors and some windows of the wagons stayed opened. On the bench of almost every wagon of our train, passengers aged four to fifteen years old sat, unaccompanied by adults.

I witnessed the enormous pain and anxiety surrounding each separation of a child from a parent. Words of love and good-byes were still in the air when the train, full of legal and "illegal"

FIG. 1. "When am I going to see my daughter again?" I am at the train station, having just been separated from my daughter, Olga, who was evacuated from Kiev along with many other children after the 1986 nuclear explosion at Chernobyl. *Photograph by Vadim Shapiro.*

passengers, slowly moved away from those who remained at the station and disappeared into the horizon. For some time, I felt abandoned and alone, with a dull pain of grief as I did not know when I would see my precious Olga again.

For the next few days, I heard similar stories of departures from my coworkers, friends, and neighbors. Everyone had a unique story, but the common thread was the chaotic and wrenching exodus from big cities and small towns in the spring and summer of 1986.

By July all children younger than seventeen years old had left Kiev, a city of over two million people. Factories, stores, and movie theaters stayed open, but playgrounds and soccer stadiums were empty. Kiev became a ghost town, though, unlike Pripyat, it was not officially listed as such. Everywhere there was fear of harm from radiation exposure.

Even with our long and challenging shifts at the hospital, we had not forgotten about Natasha since the day she offered to go in my place to an "out-of-town" consultation. She was still gone, and each day of her absence felt endless. We kept asking our boss, "What happened to Natasha?

Eventually, he got tired of hearing that question. His short answer startled us: "She is working in a dangerous zone in close proximity to the exploded reactor unit."

One morning the door of our shared workspace opened. We stared in disbelief at the stretcher and the patient entering the room. It was our missing friend. Natasha was very pale and did not greet us, even though she was safe and protected. Although we felt relieved, our misery and discomfort about her plight was undiminished.

"Start an intravenous infusion as soon as possible!"

This order sounded as a sudden cry, and the nurses rushed to follow it. They transferred Natasha from the stretcher to the couch in our office. After a few days of treatment with fluids and nutritional support, she was well enough to be discharged. An ambulance arrived, and our group assumed that she was going home.

We later discovered that, instead of taking her home, the ambulance took Natasha to the Institute of Oncology. This was a leading facility for radiation research and cancer patients receiving radiation treatment. Some of the staff also carried dosimeters, instruments used to survey radiation exposure and contamination.

Natasha told us later that she carefully removed her contaminated clothes, shoes, watch, and travel purse, which were measured by the dosimeter. A warm and thorough shower followed. She washed her long, beautiful blonde hair repeatedly, yet, despite these attempts, it continued to "glow." The decision was clear: her hair had to be cut very short. She accepted it as an order and silently agreed. We later did our best to convince her that short hair made her look younger.

Many years later I met Natasha again when I went to Kiev on an official visit. I had been invited as a speaker for the US Food and Drug Administration's Division of Counter-Terrorism at the international conference marking the twentieth anniversary of the Chernobyl nuclear disaster. Natasha had not changed much at all since I last saw her twenty years earlier.

I admired her continued energy and dedication to her career. She was a doctor of medical sciences and a senior research associate at the National Research Center for Radiation Medicine in Kiev. Her blonde hair still complemented her sparkling ocean blue eyes. We bombarded each other with questions about our personal lives, our colleagues and bosses in Ukraine and in the US, new fashions, and vacations. I sensed that Natasha did not want to revisit any painful memories. She had buried them in an impenetrable vault.

CHAPTER 4

The Human Toll of Displacement

The largest public health problem unleashed by the accident is the mental health impact.

—World Health Organization's report of the United Nations Chernobyl Forum Expert Group, 2005

E vacuation from the areas around Chernobyl and from my home city of Kiev affected each family differently.

My daughter spent over a year away from her parents and her great-grandmother, Berta, who had dedicated three years of her life helping to raise Olga. Berta was too fragile to take an overnight train or to ride for eight hours in a car to visit Olga.

However, my daughter's "exile" from us was not as difficult as that of other child-evacuees. Olga left Kiev with two of her grandparents, and they settled in Kharkov in an apartment with one of our relatives. During her very first day in the new place, my daughter built a small circle of friends.

Many children had no family members who could accompany them to a safer destination. Children of different ages were put together in large groups, and each group was assigned caregivers when they were evacuated to less radioactively dangerous areas. Those who were between eight and fifteen years of age were sent to summer camps, rest houses, sanatoria, and tourist places.

The authorities at summer camps in Ukraine refused to accept them, thinking that they were "contagious." Children from Ukraine who were evacuated to Moscow had similar experiences. The families who were asked to host the children refused to take them in, calling them "dirty." As a result, the children were moved, sometimes more than once, to different locations, and their parents lost track of them for several weeks.

The evacuations scattered families and communities throughout the Soviet Union. Many people lost their homes, jobs, friends, surroundings—everything they cared about—and they suffered deeply. Though evacuees experienced severe and prolonged periods of psychological stress after the disaster, the people most affected by the forced separations were the civil and military personnel who had to stay behind. While they dealt with the consequences of the nuclear explosion on-site, their children were evacuated to safer locations. Women seemed to experience more anxiety than men.

The town of Pripyat, designed as a model Soviet metropolis, was built in 1970 to house Chernobyl Nuclear Power Plant workers. The authorities repeatedly told the people that this city was "made just for them." Residents viewed their town as a paradise. They were enchanted by the natural beauty of the landscape, the rivers, and the fishing, as well as the abundance of berries and the mushrooms for picking in the forest. Roses and fruit trees grew everywhere.

Of course, life in this heaven on earth ended on April 26, when the city woke up to the worst nuclear disaster in history. Two days later the city was abandoned because of radioactive contamination and placed on the list of ghost towns. Evacuees from Pripyat were subsequently labeled as helpless victims and stigmatized as unclean. They were called "Chernobylites" by residents within resettlement areas.[4]

Negative effects on the developing brain, organic brain disorders, and medically unexplained physical symptoms have been found in Chernobyl-exposed populations compared to controls.[5] Many people were diagnosed with chronic fatigue syndrome, which can include persistent fatigue, muscle and joint pain, headaches, mood changes, lack of concentration and memory, cognitive deterioration, depression, and sleep disorders.

The psychological effects of Chernobyl were, and remain, widespread and profound. There were increased levels of alcoholism, apathy, depression, anxiety (including post-traumatic stress symptoms), and suicide, especially among Estonian and Lithuanian cleanup workers.[6] Exclusion zone personnel also suffered from high rates of schizophrenia,[7] as a genetic predisposition to this mental illness can be provoked by environmental stresses such as exposure to ionizing radiation.[8]

To ascertain and quantify the evidence of severe mental impact, a questionnaire was presented to the people in some of the villages in Belarus, which is about 250 miles from Chernobyl. This study revealed that one-third of the participants thought about Chernobyl almost every day, and half of the participants still thought that radiation was responsible for their mental and physical symptoms.

Wounds from every crisis present in both mental and physical forms. To lessen these effects, trained medical personnel and public officials must prepare to respond to possible damage, and to bring hope in the midst of catastrophic events. Their responses should be guided by accurate information instead of unfounded rumors. Furthermore, all nations should provide hospitality, rather than hostility, to evacuees. A government-coordinated, data-based, and transparent response would have mitigated some of the disastrous outcomes of the Chernobyl meltdown. Indeed, preparedness and transparency should be embedded in the collective conscience of every nation.

CHAPTER 5

A Radioactive Fallacy

A t the time of the Chernobyl disaster, major decisions in the USSR were not left to local authorities. They were handed down from the top. Soviet officials banned the release of any disaster-related information for days after the explosion—after which the information we received was mostly false. Even when increased radiation levels were reported in other parts of the planet, the authoritarian Soviet government refused to publicly admit the extent of the disaster. Sweden was the first country to detect dangerous levels of radioactive fallout, an alarm heard around the world.

According to news reports published long after the disaster, the initial information embargo placed by the Soviet Politburo was intended to prevent widespread panic. Though Soviet leader Mikhail S. Gorbachev urged his colleagues to make a prompt disclosure, a majority of the Politburo members decreed silence on the "embarrassing episode." The story was downplayed and the danger denied on nightly Soviet television news.

For many days the Soviet newspaper *Pravda*, which ironically means "truth" in English, printed not a word on the devastating explosion. Gorbachev finally acknowledged the disaster at an official news conference *ten days* after the event: "An accident has occurred at the Chernobyl nuclear power station. One of the atomic reactors has been damaged. Measures are being taken to eliminate the consequences of the accident. Aid is being given to the victims. A government commission has been set up."[9] Three weeks after the accident, *Pravda* acknowledged that the absence of information had contributed to public anxiety.

My learning curve was never as steep as in the months after the catastrophic event at Chernobyl. Within a few weeks of the explosion, my vocabulary expended to include such new terms as nuclear meltdown, cooling system, and radioactive rods. I learned that the Chernobyl reactors had a design that American physicist and Nobel Prize winner Hans Bethe deemed "fundamentally faulty, having a built-in instability."

On the eve of the nuclear meltdown, Chernobyl engineers experimented on Unit No. 4 to determine whether the cooling system would operate solely with energy from the reactor if the external power supply failed. The plant had no internal containment to prevent the release of radioactive material in the event of an accident. Still, to run the tests, the engineers deactivated numerous safety systems in the early morning hours of April 26. Reactor output shot up suddenly to a hundred times the normal level, causing the world's worst nuclear accident. Unit No. 4 had exploded by the time the engineers could attempt an emergency shutdown.

Everyone was unprepared for and grossly underestimated the force of steam and radioactive products that were catapulted into the atmosphere. The roof of the building blew off. Parts of the reactor core exploded like rockets through the atmosphere, spreading radiation across vast parts of Europe and the northern hemisphere. They drifted far and wide, unchecked.[10]

Helicopter pilots hovered over the burning reactor, dropping clay and dolomite to quench the blaze. The pilots and cameramen took an experimental Soviet drug, indralin, to protect them from deadly doses of radiation. Unfortunately, the drug was not effective and caused serious side effects such as nausea, vomiting, and dramatic drops in blood pressure, and it did not protect the pilots from death.[11]

After the explosion, teams of doctors from different hospitals in Kiev were deployed to the most radiation-contaminated areas in Ukraine. The government provided no protective gear or safety instructions. My supervisor told me that I would be leading a field team that consisted of three specialists: a pediatric endocrinologist (a doctor who specializes in glands and the hormones they make), a gynecologist (a specialist in the female reproductive system), and me, a pediatric hematologist (a specialist in diseases related to blood and blood-forming organs, such as bone marrow and the spleen).

Despite the fact that all the books and journals containing the word "radiation" had disappeared from library shelves, some doctors were "street smart." During a self-taught crash course in radiation, we learned that the organs most susceptible to radiation are the thyroid gland, reproductive organs in men and women, and blood cells that originate in the bone marrow. Therefore, the composition of our field team seemed appropriate in the beginning.

The endocrinologist was assigned to touch and feel the thyroid gland in each child. The role of the gynecologist was to touch and feel testicles in boys. No one suggested examining the girls' ovaries. As a hematologist, I was expected to touch and examine lymph nodes located on both sides of the neck, under both arms, and in the groin. Neither our supervisors nor any of our medical staff members knew then that visible or palpable changes in the thyroid gland, ovaries, or lymphatic nodes would occur only years after the exposure. We believed that our mission was timely and important. However, this belief changed after we spent a few days examining hundreds of children who lived in the contaminated areas of Ukraine.

During the day, our team of three doctors worked in one of the school buildings, assisted by nurses from local clinics and hospitals who directed the patient flow and recorded the results of each child's physical exam. We provided the nurses with abbreviated versions of assessments to save time so that each of us could focus on our current patient. The line of children seemed endless—child after child, child after child.

At the end of the second day, the endocrinologist started to cry. The young physician had not examined as many patients in her entire career as she had in those two days. My blunt question, "What's wrong with you?" brought more tears to her eyes.

She started talking through her tears: "I cannot take it anymore. There is no end. I want to go home! Send me home!"

I ignored her plaintive cries and turned my head to find the gynecologist. The doctor's head was looking down, and his hands were touching a little boy's testicles. My colleague finished his exam. The boy pulled his pants up and ran out the door. The gynecologist looked straight through me, and he too said, "I cannot take it anymore. There is no end. I want to go home! Send me home!"

These revelations stunned me. *Deal with this, now,* commanded my internal voice. *We need to come up with a more efficient way of examining patients.* And I did.

I laid out a plan to expedite our process. I said, "From now on, follow these directions: Start with only boys entering the room in single file. After they form a line, I will instruct, 'Hands up! Pants down!' After the boys obey, we will start moving down the line where the kids are standing.

"You, as the endocrinologist, go first; touch, perhaps feel, the thyroid gland in each boy and quickly move to the next, until you reach the end of the line."

I did not have to explain to the gynecologist. My colleague smiled for the first time in three days, then he chuckled as he ran from one boy to the next.

I was the last one on my "marathon" team to complete a partial physical exam. I tried to be gentle; however, the result was the opposite. The majority of boys giggled while I was lightly touching the lymphatic nodes under their arms. My next move—to feel nodes in their groin area—caused uncontrollable laughter.

Our team transformed the tragedy of the procedure into a comedy show! Assuaged, we remained focused on the orchestrated exams until we departed for the day.

The boys told their peers about their fun experience, and the word spread so that the rest of the schoolchildren competed for their turn to enter the exam room first. Another day passed, with streamlined evaluations and upbeat spirits on the part of the participants. At the end of the day, my two colleagues and I proceeded to our designated area for rest and recuperation.

As the leader of the field team, I had the "honor" to stay in "Lenin's Corner"—a room that existed in every public place across the entire Soviet Union. Lenin's rooms were adorned with images of Lenin, serving as shrines to the former leader. Such memorabilia were displayed in the Palaces of Young Pioneers, Palaces of Culture and Art, and sports arenas, as well as prison cells.

My solitary room was in a remote part of the hospital. When I first entered the room, I was not surprised to discover that the other "occupant" was Lenin! The leader of the Bolshevik Party, the first leader of the government that took over Russia in 1917, was staring at me from each wall and from each corner. I gazed at Vladimir Lenin's portraits, a photograph of Lenin, a series of Lenin-related collages, and busts of Lenin, each intended to further Lenin's mission to inspire a socialist revolution led by the working class.

Wanting to keep a distance from these items in the room, I headed straight for the bathroom to wash my hands after a full day taking care of children. What I discovered in the bathroom still haunts me thirty-three years later: the bathtub was filled with water of an intensely purple color, and it had a strong unpleasant smell. I immediately recognized that the color change and the odor of the water were due to potassium permanganate, an inorganic chemical compound that is used as a medication. In the absence of topical disinfectant, potassium permanganate was used for cleaning wounds and treating inflammation of the skin.

Why did someone decide to add permanganate to tap water?

I suspected the answer, and it made me uneasy, so I decided to seek validation. I walked over and visited my two colleagues. There was no bathtub in their facility.

"Guys, I need your opinion on the following," I said, and I briefly described the scary looking bathtub water and its odor of rotten eggs.

One of my colleagues, a PhD in endocrinology, said: "Tap water is highly radioactive in this area, and adding permanganate to it will reduce the level of its radioactivity."

"What do you think, Oksana?" I asked my other team member.

"I think that Alex is right," answered the gynecologist.

I was stunned. Contrary to popular belief, potassium permanganate is useless for reducing radiation levels in water. I thought, *How could two intelligent and knowledgeable doctors disregard the obvious?*

I was caught in a bind. As the team leader, my duty was to maintain the party line that everything was safe, yet we all knew that the water must be contaminated. I replied with a confidence I did not feel: "No one measured the tap water for radiation content; therefore, we do not know the level of radiation in it." It seemed that my colleagues agreed. I continued, "The purple stuff added to the water must be to protect it from possible growth of different bacteria." The silence that greeted my pronouncement meant neither no nor yes.

I was caught in the web of lies and deceit. I had swallowed misinformation disseminated from the top of the Soviet government ladder. For weeks, I replayed in my head government voices: "You must tell the population living in the areas affected by radiation that everything is fine. Staying outside and collecting mushrooms and berries is not dangerous to their health. If you do not follow these orders, you are committing a crime. And punishment for this will be to lose your job permanently."

I reiterated my statement, emphasizing that permanganate was not intended to diminish the radiation, but to kill harmful bacteria in the water. Instead of stepping off the ladder of lies, I chose to continue doing my duties for fear of losing my job and career forever. Our silent conclusion from this whole episode, however, was unanimous. None of us wanted to consume any food or drink containing water from the nearby areas.

On another of my visits to a heavily contaminated area, I was introduced to what I called "The Chernobyl Diet." A warm greeting awaited me at a small hospital in a village where silence had not yet been mandated. Doctors and nurses were excited by the visit from a physician from the top children's hospital in Kiev.

Ukrainian mushrooms are frequent ingredients in soup and other traditional dishes, and rumors circulated that mushrooms could clean up everything from oil spills to nuclear meltdowns. It was even suggested that mushrooms be planted in the woods across Ukraine to absorb radiation and decontaminate the dangerous zones.

What I saw as I toured the small hospital might have made me laugh before the nuclear meltdown but not in its aftermath. In the back of a room in the village hospital, a shiny new autoclave stood on a table. Autoclaves are used to sterilize surgical equipment, laboratory instruments, and other materials. While autoclaves use steam to kill bacteria, spores, and germs that are resistant to water and detergents, pressure cookers use steam to cook food.

A nurse, apparently noting the similarities between the two, assumed they served identical functions. She collected mushrooms in the local woods, threaded them onto a thin rope, and hung them between the autoclave's walls, unwittingly creating a new recipe for "radioactive mushrooms 'dried' in an autoclave." I was under orders not to reveal that the radiation content in Ukrainian mushrooms was eight times over the levels safe for human consumption. Horrified, I told the hospital staff that using the autoclave for food was unsanitary and asked them to remove and discard the mushrooms immediately.

The next year during my visit to the same hospital, I was in the car with the driver. He abruptly pulled over and lowered the window, drawing my attention to a gigantic mushroom. I stared at the monstrous fungus and wondered, *Is this nature reclaiming its territory in the aftermath of a nuclear disaster, or did the mushroom grow so large because of radiation?*

Many people lost their source of livelihood overnight in this primarily agricultural region. Farmers with no safe produce to sell attached fake labels to the baskets of berries that they collected in the woods around Kiev and other cities. Even though many of them could barely pronounce the word "radioactive," they knew that the magic word "clean" in quotation marks must be displayed on the label for their produce to be considered safe and ready for consumption. Corruption and fabrication of "clean" labels flourished in the forest and, regrettably, in the laboratory.

CHAPTER 6

Doctors on Call

I continued my work in the affected areas. From on-the-job training and a self-taught crash course on radiation basics, I learned that, unlike burns from high temperatures (thermal burns), radiation burns are not immediately visible on the skin. However, a few weeks after the explosion when I worked at one of the highly contaminated areas near Chernobyl, I witnessed an episode that turned upside down my belief in the science behind this phenomenon.

One patient required evacuation by air from a remote area to a hospital in Kiev. The helicopter landed on the grass, then two men grabbed stretchers and ran barefoot across a short stretch of sand to pick up the patient. When the two men returned, the skin of their feet was bright red. It looked as though they were wearing red socks. I touched the sand, and it felt only slightly warm, so the burns could not have been caused by a high temperature.

For many years after witnessing this, I searched for answers to this question: How could radiation burns appear on the skin immediately after exposure without any latent period? The mystery was solved only a few years ago by one of the top scientists in the field of radiation biology. He explained that the friction of skin rubbing against the radioactive sand particles caused the immediate burn.

Belatedly, I also learned that some of the skin burns could have been avoided. On the evening of the explosion, the night shift workers at the Chernobyl power station were still wearing uniforms soaked in radioactive water. These workers did not have keys for the lockers that stored clean and dry clothes. Only the morning shift workers had access to the lockers. As a result, the night shift stayed for many hours in clothes drenched in radiation-contaminated water. The burns they suffered were attributable to insufficient knowledge and preparedness, a lethal legacy.

Though I occasionally treated adults, most of my first-responder work was with children. One assignment was obtaining bone marrow samples from children who lived in a highly contaminated area in Ukraine. My orders from the head of the Pediatric Hematology Unit consisted of two parts: first, obtain bone marrow from healthy children, and second, freeze and store the bone marrow cells. No explanation was given.

I typically drew bone marrow samples for diagnosing hematological malignancies as well as nonmalignant diseases in children. In my experience, a bone marrow exam was performed if blood tests were abnormal or didn't provide enough information about a suspected problem.

I detected no medical problems in any of the young patients who came for the physical exam that day. The children appeared healthy as they played with toys, and they made silly faces when Doctor Alla asked them to take their shirts off.

What came next terrified the little ones. Medical personnel held the children still as I used a thin needle to draw bone marrow from their sternum—without local anesthetics, which were not available.

After each ordeal was over, parents hugged their crying, traumatized children and carried them away from the operating room. When I had completed these interventions, I expected my boss to explain why they were necessary, but no explanation was offered.

Thirty years later I learned, in an unexpected way, why he ordered this procedure. When I worked at the National Institutes of Health (NIH) in Bethesda, Maryland, I collaborated on Chernobyl-related projects with former colleagues, including my former supervisor, who worked at the Radiobiology Institute in Kiev. I was astounded to learn that bone marrow samples obtained and preserved for more than fifteen years in Ukraine had recently been added to the NIH marrow sample repository.

Even though the children I drew bone marrow samples from appeared to be asymptomatic, they could have been exposed to low doses of radiation (< 1 Gy), which can cause changes on the chromosomal level. This chromosomal instability is the hallmark, or the precursor, of cancer.[12] By employing new techniques using "old" bone marrow samples, experts have been able to identify changes in chromosomes indicating radiation damage and to advance efforts to predict the future occurrence of cancers.

My boss's vision and intuition led to his decision to obtain those bone marrow samples. As a result, three decades later we were able to answer many questions. Cooperation such as this between countries is critical. Other specimens obtained at Chernobyl are currently used at NIH to study the effects of a variety of doses of radiation on human health.

On one of our field trips to an area with significant radiation contamination, we were sent to a hospital in Narodichi town, located around forty-two miles from Chernobyl. One day my mom, who lived in Kiev, called the nurses' station at the hospital to leave a message for me. She asked the nurse who answered the call to let me know that my grandmother had cooked dinner for all three members of my team and that my mom would bring it to us.

I happily accepted this kind gesture. My colleagues were excited at the prospect of enjoying a delicious meal. Mom had good reason to be concerned about the quality of food in the area we were deployed to. She was a prominent physician at the Institute of Kidney Diseases in Kiev and was well known throughout Ukraine. In the absence of information about the area where our team would be working, she rightly suspected that our workplace area was in the "hot zone."

My mom traveled two hours on a public bus to reach the village where the hospital was located, then walked from the bus station carrying heavy bags laden with our homemade meals. She reached the hospital at midday, hoping to meet me there. However, all three of us were working in different locations and would not come back to the hospital until late. The last bus back to Kiev was leaving soon, so Mom was in a rush to unload her bags and to transfer food to the refrigerator. She explained the goal of her visit to the nurse, and asked permission to use the fridge.

The head nurse looked at my mom with surprise and asked, "Why did you bring this food from Kiev for your daughter and the other doctors? We have enough food to feed them all."

My mom said, "I don't want doctors who are taking care of many children in the area to eat food contaminated with radiation. They are working long hours without any protective clothes, and they don't know the dose of radiation they are receiving. Radiation levels in this area are dangerously high, especially in the food that they eat.

I am trying to protect them. If I can do anything to decrease their exposure, I want to do it."

My mom's honest response sparked a furious reaction from the head nurse: "What about us? What about our children? What you are doing is selfish and unfair."

"Please, take the food," said my mother. "If the doctors stay healthy, they will be of more help to their patients."

The nurse angrily burst out, "If you leave this food here, your daughter will be in trouble. I will report to her bosses that her mom is trying to protect her while the whole population is eating radiation contaminated food."

Throughout her life, my mom learned that bosses don't like "violation" of any rules established by Soviet leaders. She had years of experience obeying the rules in order to keep her job as a physician, about which she was so passionate. Therefore, she did not want me to commit the "crime" of eating food that was not polluted with radiation. She knew what the punishment would be for this transgression.

"Where can I throw all it away? I have to walk back to the bus. It's getting dark, and I don't want to take all this food back home." My mom never told me in detail what answer and directions she received from the head nurse in response to her final question.

I bumped into my mom as she was leaving the hospital. She was late for the last bus and told me only the highlights of this story. Mom looked very tired. She nodded toward her bags. They were light, without food, just empty dishes. We hugged briefly and Mom hurried to the bus stop.

I was exhausted after twelve hours of intense work examining patients. I knew that after a few hours of sleep I would go to the laboratory, where technicians were staining the blood smears they had obtained from patients during the day. Blood cell counts were performed without use of a machine. We strained our eyes for many hours during those sleepless nights, counting blood cells, unaware that elsewhere in the world blood work was done by machine.

I skipped the hospital dinner and went to bed. I was thinking of my mom having had one more painful life lesson: by trying to help others you hurt yourself. We can "reclassify" the truth, but nobody can control our minds or stifle our speech when we are ready to reveal damage caused by silence. And the truth did eventually emerge. According to the Cabinet of Ministers of Ukraine, Narodichi was evacuated. In that town and surrounding areas, radiation affected some 93,000 people, 20,000 of them children.[13]

CHAPTER 7

Red Wine Improves Doctor-Patient Communications

After my field trip, I returned to Children's Hospital, where we then evaluated and treated hundreds of evacuated children of different ages from Pripyat and nearby villages. As we struggled to help pediatric patients, medical personnel at the hospitals for adults were dealing with the overflow of patients from the contaminated areas. Many pediatricians who had not examined or treated adults since medical school were sometimes summoned and pressed into service as "noncertified" internal medicine (adult) doctors. I was one of them.

My first visit to the hospital for adults in Kiev was memorable. I entered the room where eight men, all former workers from the Chernobyl nuclear power station, were staying for their evaluation and treatment. These middle-aged men seemed tired and were reluctant to make eye contact or talk. Then I noticed one man sitting on the corner bed, holding a few sheets of paper that were folded like a book. He waved to me with an inviting smile.

In my career thus far, I had not begun a medically-oriented discussion with a person older than sixteen years of age. Therefore, I followed a "cheat sheet" that I had kept in my mind from my days at medical school. I asked, "What are your complaints?"

My patient responded, "What are you talking about, girl? What complaints? I am grateful to the driver of the ambulance who brought me to this hospital—no complaints whatsoever!"

This response was an icebreaker. No inhibition or tension remained between us. Our communication turned into a lively and interesting sidebar conversation. My patient handed his workplace protocols to me: "This is our manual, which we had at the nuclear power station at Chernobyl. We had to read it before we accepted any job there. One of our favorite recommendations is that in case of radiation emergency we should"—he paused, and looked like a dreamer—"we should drink red wine!"

I tried not to laugh. I would never hear such jokes from my pediatric patients. Welcome to the reality of dealing with adults!

"May I see the reference to drinking red wine in case of radiation emergency?" I asked him politely.

His answer shocked me: "After the accident the corresponding part of the manual was removed."

I looked intently into my patient's eyes. He was serious and seemed slightly disappointed. I stopped the conversation, but his answer continued to bother me.

After work I went to my parents' apartment. I wanted to mobilize three generations of my family to go to the grocery store and to buy as many cases of red wine as my family members could carry. We entered the store and were stunned to find empty wine shelves staring back at us. We looked at each other in dismay and disbelief and left the store—further proof that rumors spread as fast as radiation.

Currently, scientists in the US are investigating a component called resveratrol, which is present in red wine. If approved as a drug, it might protect human cells from the harmful effects of radiation.

However, according to the developers of this product, "Someone would have to drink approximately 720 bottles of wine to match the results of the compound they have created. By the time someone drank that much wine," they joked, "they wouldn't have to worry about radiation anymore."[14]

There is evidence that resveratrol can modify the behavior of cells in response to radiation-induced damage. Studies using mice have demonstrated the protective effects of resveratrol against radiation-induced intestinal injury, which is a potential cause of death after high-dose radiation exposure. Resveratrol has relatively low toxicity and has been widely used as a food supplement for management of various human health conditions.[15]

Another potential application of resveratrol is to protect normal human cells from damage during radiation treatment intended to kill cancer cells, and resveratrol may also be useful in the case of radiological accidents.[16]

PART II

A Harrowing Journey from Statelessness to US Citizenship

CHAPTER 8

Departure from Decades of Prejudice and Lies

In an electricity or water disappearance claim, there is always a Jew to blame.

—RUSSIAN FOLKLORE

In April 1986, the twin traumas of my life coincided. While responding to the Chernobyl disaster, I reached the defining moment, the tipping point, in my lifelong battle against state-sponsored, institutionalized anti-Semitism.

Since I was a child, I understood that persecution of Jewish people was an established fact of life. Members of my immediate family had prepared me for it early by sharing their life stories. My grandmother Berta's memories frequently went back to World War II. In fact, Berta and people of her generation divided their lives into "before" and "after" the war.

"Why are you talking about this, Grandma?" I asked her. "The war was over many years ago."

She replied that "war had such a horrible effect on our family, our country, and society, I will never forget it."

"Tell me more about it, Grandma. I want to be a doctor and treat people when I grow up. I don't want to die in war."

She replied sadly, "Yes, but doctors also died in war. One of your aunts, who was a dentist, died. Her name was Stacya. She was young, good-looking, and worked in one of the clinics in Kiev. She had blonde hair and blue eyes, like yours. When the Germans invaded Kiev in September 1941, the Nazis made mass arrests and executed Jews who lived in the city. Some Ukrainians collaborated with the Nazis, helping to identify places where Jewish people worked or lived."

Berta explained that, one day in September, Stacya became sick. She was running a high fever and could not go to work. Her neighbors, a Ukrainian couple who lived next door, heard that some Ukrainians had betrayed their Jewish neighbors. They offered to let Stacya stay at their apartment, hoping that, if Germans came, Stacya would be protected. The wife was even going to show her passport and pretend that her Ukrainian last name belonged to Stacya.

I was excited and impatient to hear the happy ending of this story. Grandma looked away from me and almost whispered the rest.

"Two Nazis broke into their apartment, quickly crossed the small room, and approached the bed where Stacya was lying. The blanket covered her body, almost reaching her eyes. She appeared to be asleep. The Nazi reached for the blanket with his gun and pulled the cover down."

"What happened after that, Grandma? Did they realize that she was sick and leave?" My young mind was ready to close this chapter. My grandma was holding her words, like she was not ready for closure.

Carefully weighing her words, she said, "Stacya was sweating, and it looked like her fever broke. She half opened her eyes and started talking. Every word that she pronounced was in Yiddish."

I wanted to close my ears so as not to hear the rest and almost jumped up to run away. Instead I froze.

"The Nazi pulled Stacya down to the floor. She continued muttering. One of the Nazis pushed her outside the door. With the help of the other one, they dragged Stacya to the car, shut the door, and took off."

That was not the end of the story. For years I thought that my grandmother did not know what ultimately happened to Stacya.

When I grew older, my parents told me about Babi Yar, a ravine outside of Kiev that became the site of massacres carried out by German forces during their campaign in Ukraine against the Soviet Union in World War II. The first and best documented of the massacres took place on September 29–30, 1941, killing approximately 33,771 Jews. Stacya was one of them.[17]

I had often heard that history repeats itself, though I never really thought about whether this was true. Retrospectively, I realized that some of the stories I had heard and the pictures I had seen as a child resonated with my current life. Just the frames around them were different.

In the spring of 1985, rumors started spreading throughout Kiev that a violent riot aimed at Jews, called a pogrom, was imminent. The day and time of this massacre were not identified. Sympathetic friends, neighbors, relatives, and coworkers, though spread throughout the city, gathered to provide emotional support for each other. One moment I felt like a fighter; the next moment I felt paralyzed with fear for my family and myself.

Some people warned of impending destruction of Jewish homes and business by the "pogromers," prompting tens of thousands of Jews to think about hiding.

I had known the word "pogrom" and its meaning for many years. It was used in tales that my grandmother told me. Berta wanted me to know our family history, but did not want to tell me the harshest stories. Although she told me about the notorious pogroms that took place during the nineteenth and early twentieth centuries in Kiev and many other cities, she played down some scenes. "Some good people were hiding Jews at their houses. When the pogromers appeared, the Jews went into hiding. The bad people found no one and went away."

As an adult I tried to shake off the effect of these chronicles and to create an optimistic present. I told myself, "We are in the mid-1980s, a time of significant scientific and medical discoveries, innovative products and technologies. We have satellites and spaceships, and our soccer team is the best in the world. Pogroms belong to the past." My internal voice disagreed and ominously suggested that the human beings of the present aren't much different from those of the past.

After my early morning pep talk, I would drop off my daughter at my parents' house and go to work. As a pediatrician, I tried to concentrate on my little patients and their health problems. The complexity of this job took my mind off the possibility of anti-Jewish violence.

The phone in our office rang. One of my colleagues picked it up. "It's for you," she said, handing me the receiver.

My next-door neighbor in our apartment block, Nina, who was a Christian, was on the line. The lack of even a short greeting signaled her stress: "Alla, pick up Olga from your parents' house, but don't go to your apartment with her. My family would like you to stay with us for as long as it takes for this pogrom nightmare to go away." She continued, "Tell me what you might need from your apartment, and I will get it for you."

Tears filled my eyes, but I did not try to stop myself from crying. Because of the grace in Nina's words, I felt safer than I had for a long time. We spent three days and nights with Nina and her caring family. Then the rumors over the upcoming anti-Jewish violence quietly disappeared and our fears subsided. We understood the meaning of true friendship: to be able to count on one another over the years. Even after our family departed from the USSR four years later, we maintained our friendship with Nina and her family.

We were fortunate to be reunited over twenty years later in 2006, when I attended an international conference in Kiev dedicated to the twentieth Chernobyl anniversary. My presentation focused on the development of medical countermeasures against radiation exposure and their potential use in humans.

I was booked to stay at a nice hotel in the center of Kiev. Instead, I spent two nights with Nina and her family, in that same apartment where I was in hiding so many years ago. My extended family was together again. Its members stood up against anti-Semitism, just as my Aunt Stacya's friends had over four decades before. For thousands of years righteous individuals like Nina have helped Jewish people survive through exiles, persecutions, and assimilation.

I grew up during a time of turmoil in the USSR that seemed unlikely to end. Attacks on Jews were prevalent, and the organized practice of Judaism was unsafe and nearly impossible. During my youth there was only one synagogue in Kiev, a city with a population of over two million. Two older synagogues had been closed and transformed into a puppet theater and a movie theater. The last open synagogue had a state-of-the-art surveillance system. Anyone still active in the workforce who attended the synagogue was asked for an ID and their work and home addresses. This information was passed on to the appropriate supervisor at their place of work. Consequences varied from a warning, to a demand never to attend the synagogue again, or to termination from work. Only the elderly, presumably retired, and children were spared these indignities.

There were also "unwritten" Jewish quotas in place at most academic institutes in the Soviet Union, intended to limit the number of Jewish students. Accordingly, my parents drilled into me from an early age that I would not attend a good college if I did not excel throughout elementary, middle, and high school. I took this to heart and ended my precollege schooling with all A's. (I mention my academic record not to boast but to illustrate the barriers that confronted Jews.)

My passion for medicine became apparent at a tender age. My mother, Neli, was an acclaimed physician in Kiev who specialized in kidney diseases. She infused in me her love of this work and privately hoped that her daughter would embrace the same profession. In an early childhood photograph (see fig. 2), my love of medicine is already evident. Even as a young child, treatments and cures flew through my mind, and I envisioned a future taking care of sick children. Eventually, I did follow in my mother's footsteps.

FIG. 2. As a five-year-old doctor, I examine a baby doll—my first patient—while my friends look on. *Photograph from the author's family collection.*

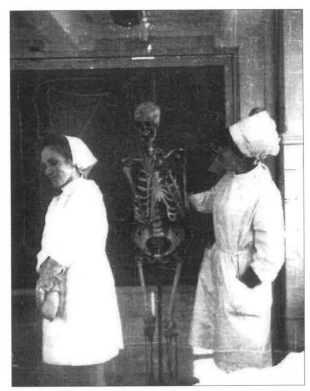

FIG. 3. My first year of medical school, 1971, in Kiev. I am on the left, looking away from the skeleton. *Photograph from the author's family collection.*

When I started medical school after high school (as was the practice in the USSR), I was one of two Jews in a class of over 150 students. In my first year at the best medical school in Ukraine, I experienced religious discrimination. At the beginning of the school year, the dean announced that there would be a competition for academic excellence. Students were divided into groups of twelve to fifteen. In order to win, all members of a group had to finish the year with straight A's.

The prize was a week-long, all-expenses-paid trip to Poland—truly a treat because few Soviet citizens were allowed to leave the country. My group won. The announcement was greeted with enthusiastic applause and hugs. But the jubilation was short-lived. It was immediately followed by a retraction from the dean's office. After a quick review of the names of the winners, the department unanimously agreed that sending abroad a group of students that included one member with an obviously Jewish surname would be "politically unacceptable." The joy of all the winners was dashed as the hard-earned prize trip to Poland was cancelled without further explanation or reward.

I felt like an outcast, guilty of something over which I had no control. Despite assurances and support from every student in my group, I was ashamed of my name, and it took a long time for me to regain hope for the future.

After completing medical school, I successfully defended my PhD dissertation in the field of hematology. I then began working and gaining recognition as a pediatric hematologist. At one of the few international conferences hosted by the Scientific Society in Kiev, copies of the latest scientific journals published in the USSR were on display. Printouts of the articles with summaries in English were available for the attendees. One of the journals included my research and clinical work on children with acute leukemia, complete with results and medical conclusions.

The study was groundbreaking: the results had been assessed using cutting-edge laboratory assays and blood screening procedures, which allowed more precise interpretation of data and provided greater insight into the prognosis of the disease. I was proud of this accomplishment, the first of its kind in my field.

A few weeks after the conference, I received a letter from an American clinical researcher who had attended the conference. He requested the full edition of the journal that contained my article. I felt the sort of pride that I had experienced when the hard-won trip to Poland was announced. But government discrimination again diminished my accomplishment. To send the journal to the clinical center in the US, I had to obtain permission through the bureaucratic chain of command.

The decision to decline that permission came from so-called Department One. This unit had an office in every large enterprise and institution of the Soviet Union. The job description for Department One employees was simple: they were responsible for secrecy and political security in the workplace. They reported to the KGB any perceived wrongdoing; they observed the movements and inferred the motives of every employee. In my case, Department One threatened to notify the KGB of my "wrong intention." The unspoken reason for Department One's refusal to grant permission to send my article to the United States was that I was Jewish. This instance of endemic anti-Semitism was no less painful to me than that first episode of discrimination that I experienced at medical school.

Though such discrimination pervaded the Soviet Union, after years of intense training and study I realized my dreams and became a physician at one of the largest children's hospitals in Kiev. I worked long hours and loved spending time with my little patients more than with my adult friends. I needed to have children under my care as much as they needed me. But the massive nuclear explosion at Chernobyl incinerated my dreams and smashed my future into smithereens. It made me re-evaluate every aspect of my life as I frantically searched for—and found—a new direction: helping the victims of radiation.

In the aftermath of Chernobyl, I wanted to understand and treat the resulting radiation damage to people and to educate other physicians about it. My experience at the front lines of the catastrophe showed me that doctors lacked even basic knowledge of the impact of radiation on humans. Moreover, everyone had unfounded opinions about this invisible threat.

Like others in our inner circle of pediatric hematologists, I was aware that our supervisor, the professor, was making a crucial decision. He selected three doctors from our department to follow him as staff members at the newly opened Institute of Radiation Biology in Kiev. We held our breath as we waited to learn who would be the "chosen" pediatricians.

One day the professor called me to his office. He closed the door, and with a mysterious expression on his face, paused, then said, "You will be one of three doctors who will soon start working at the Research Center for Radiation Medicine. I have been appointed as the director of the institute, and you will be one of my senior staff members."

I felt a surge of excitement, but was speechless with emotion. The professor continued, "You will start working at the new institute soon. I just need a final approval from the minister of health. Lots of responsibilities for you," he added with a smile.

"The more, the better!" I fired back.

I started counting weeks, then days, then hours, but no further word or confirmation from the professor was forthcoming. After about a month of silence since our last conversation, I sensed some unusual notes in the professor's voice. Our daily discussion about the patients seemed as professional and personal as before, yet I sensed that he knew something that he didn't want to share with me.

Finally, I confronted him. "Could you please tell me when I am going to start my new job?"

The professor's face turned white; he looked frightened and worried. He took my hand into his and held his other hand to his heart. He said, "I had a meeting with the minister of health a few weeks ago. We discussed three candidates, including you, for future positions at the new institute. First, I presented two of your colleagues: Natasha and Katya. Without any hesitation the minister approved both. He recalled Natasha's trip to the highly radioactive area around Chernobyl. The second candidate, Katya, had a 'clean' history too. Her dad was a high-ranking KGB civilian employee. Then I mentioned your candidacy. The minister read your last name, Shapiro, out loud and then asked, 'And *what* is this?' He didn't even ask 'who' is this? just 'what' is this?"

The minister could not even envision a Jewish doctor as a senior staff member at the premier institute in Ukraine. He felt ashamed to have this "dirty" doctor as an applicant for a position there.

My future died in front of me. I did not respond, just carefully withdrew my hand from the professor's firm grasp. I left his office and didn't look back. My thoughts were compressed as they were in the first days after the nuclear catastrophe. My before-Chernobyl stories began to intertwine with the ones after Chernobyl.

I represented the "young generation," which now confronted the same discrimination that my family had experienced. The grim lesson I learned was that, as long as I lived in the Soviet Union, I would have to accept the targeting of Jews for no reason other than that they were Jews. My daughter would have to face the same grim reality.

My grandmother Berta's life had been one long struggle against discrimination. In the 1950s, her husband, Yakov, had been imprisoned for six months. His arrest was based on the allegation that he had been "hiring too many Jews to work at the glass factory" where he was chief engineer. Yakov survived a heart attack while in prison and overcame the false accusation.

After his release, he felt that the values he treasured about his country had been swept away like trash—*just as a fine glass vase from the factory where Grandpa worked goes from treasure to fragments the moment it is shattered,* I thought. Yakov's health deteriorated and he succumbed to a second heart attack at the age of fifty-eight while climbing the stairs to his office.

After my grandfather's death in 1959, my heartbroken grandmother remained strong despite her loss. For many years she continued to support our family, helping us to continue working and studying. It was her resilience and love that gave us the courage to leave our homeland in 1989 and begin our long journey into an unknown future.

My mother, Neli, like my grandmother before her, felt the sting of anti-Semitism. My mom's medical career began during the darkest years of the Soviet regime. As a young physician and researcher, my mom was preparing to defend her dissertation. When she was close to presenting her data before the medical board, shocking news came: Neli was wrongfully accused of being associated with a few prominent intellectual and political dissidents. My mom was identified as the "go-between" for her mentor, Dr. Max Gubergritz, and his colleague, Dr. Miron Vovsi, a renowned physician who treated many members of the Soviet government and leading generals of the Red Army in the Kremlin Hospital. Dr. Vovsi was arrested, along with Stalin's personal physician.

In that same year, news of a chain of events that became known as the Doctors' Plot rocked the country and the entire world. In the so-called Doctors' Plot, nine Soviet doctors (seven of them Jewish) were accused of espionage and of terrorist activities against the active leaders of the Soviet government. Seven of the doctors were cleared and immediately released, but two had died at the hands of their jailers.[18]

My mother was fortunate to escape prosecution. Even so, the rest of her professional life was plagued by her "Jewishness." After Stalin's death in 1953, *Pravda* announced that a reexamination of the case showed the charges against the doctors were false, and their confessions extracted by torture. In 1953 an official in the Ministry of State Security and some police officers were executed for their part in fabricating the cases against the doctors.[19]

My mom successfully defended her dissertation and added a well-deserved PhD next to her MD when she was twenty-five years old. Despite such a bright beginning, my mother faced religious discrimination throughout her career as a Soviet physician. She was an acclaimed specialist in kidney diseases in Kiev. Considered an expert in what is now the Republic of Ukraine, she was at the cutting edge of scientific and clinical discoveries in diagnosing and treating kidney conditions. During this time, hemodialysis or, more simply, dialysis (the process of using a machine to purify the blood of a person whose kidneys are not working properly) was developed, revolutionizing the field of renal medicine. Patients with kidney failure were successfully treated with the system, which performed slow continuous filtration of blood to clear the plasma of toxic substances.[20]

At the First International Conference on Hemodialysis, held in Kiev in the early 1970s, my mother was permitted to attend as a silent guest only. Soviet officials forbade my mom from presenting her groundbreaking work on her treatment of patients on dialysis. No explanation was given as to *why* she could not present the results of her research. But everyone understood the unspoken, ugly truth that her last name, when announced, would scream, "Jewish!" For other Russians and Ukrainians, last names were just another fact of life, but for the Goldsteins, Shapiros, and other Jews, an invisible Star of David blazoned at every introduction. So as not to tarnish the litany of Russian names, the Soviet authorities removed "politically incorrect" names, rendering them invisible to international colleagues and the public.

Despite Neli's impeccable work and reputation, she was never promoted to a higher position based on merit in her profession. Being Jewish precluded it. To put it in medical terms, a "syndrome of official anti-Semitism" in the Soviet Union reached new heights. My mom was banned repeatedly from presenting her research at domestic and international scientific conferences. Her work was presented by others whose non-Jewish last names were "acceptable." My mother applied fourteen times for a scientific position in a few clinical research institutes in Kiev. She tried her luck in some of the places more than once. Despite her skills and her medical and scientific degrees, she was rejected. Her last name, Melman, and "line 5" in her passport, indicating Jewish "nationality," did not meet hiring criteria in the USSR. Finally, Yuri Yedinuy, one of Mom's friends from medical school who became a director of one of the prestigious institutes in Kiev, hired my mother. For over three decades she worked at that institute, where she is still remembered for her brilliance and passion for medicine, not for her Jewish surname.

Despite all the adversity my mother had overcome in her life, when we left the Soviet Union in 1989, she viewed quitting her job and leaving behind dear friends and her career as a specialist in nephrology as something tantamount to abandoning a beloved but unruly child.

The April 1986 disaster in at the Chernobyl nuclear power station in Ukraine was a major reason why my family left the Soviet Union. The government had knowingly ignored its responsibilities to protect its people, and to warn the surrounding nations of the dangerously high levels of radiation in their atmosphere and food chain. The lies and cover-ups in the months after the Chernobyl disaster finally broke any remnant of trust that I may have had in the government, along with my hopes for a safe and secure future in the Soviet Union. As my family prepared for our passage to America, we pictured ourselves wandering in the dark, facing the great unknown, and dealing with endless uncertainties.

The final decision to emigrate was made at a family gathering. My husband and I took the lead, laying out a plan and a time for the move. Without hesitation, each adult family member began the complex formal process of leaving the Soviet Union.

I will never forget the tense time just before our departure from Kiev. Three weeks before we were due to leave, my grandmother had a stroke. She was hospitalized and remained unconscious for several days. When she regained consciousness, her first question was, "Am I going with you? You are not leaving me here, are you?"

My mother's immediate response was, "Yes, Mom, you are going. We all are going."

Berta, who had barely started showing signs of recovery, was unafraid to undertake this difficult journey. She had chosen to leave with her family, though some of her friends stayed behind when their loved ones fled.

Our family also faced difficult choices regarding my father, Yefim. He was a decorated World War II veteran. He had earned his engineering diploma after the war ended, then worked for many years in the aviation industry, and subsequently in the shipping industry as a civil engineer.

Over the years, my father had developed a growing mistrust of the ideas for which he had risked his life during World War II. His faith in the ideals of socialism, which had gained momentum among citizens of the Soviet Union, started to collapse. My dad no longer believed in the propaganda that the Soviet media was spewing. Everything he had sacrificed for was gone, only to be replaced by the new "progressive" slogans. Yefim was ready to leave. Physically, however, he would probably be too frail to take the long journey.

Although only sixty-seven years old, my father suffered from chronic illness, and by the time the family decided to emigrate, his health had deteriorated significantly. After much discussion, we faced the harsh reality that his chances of surviving the long and unknown journey, with its uncertainties and potential obstacles, were slim. Yefim was the first to suggest that he stay behind in Kiev until the family was settled in the US, when he would fly directly from Kiev to Washington to join us. This decision was painful for my family, but it was the only sensible choice.

As things turned out, fate made the choice for us. Ten days before our departure, my dad collapsed in the kitchen of our apartment and died of a pulmonary embolism. A blood clot had traveled from his leg to his lungs. Coping with his unexpected death added an enormous burden of loss to the sadness and stress of leaving. My family members each managed the grieving process as best they could under the circumstances.

CHAPTER 9

Fear and Fortitude

D uring the post–World War II era, the Soviet Union imposed severe restrictions on travel abroad for ordinary citizens (but not for Soviet leaders and their relatives). Nor were we allowed access to information about other countries. Therefore, my family set off with little knowledge of America.

In true communist fashion, the Soviet government had launched a propaganda campaign to convince citizens that Soviet TV programs *about* going abroad would satisfy their wanderlust. The most popular of these shows was *The Travelers' Club*, which followed the adventures of a few high-ranking government officials that had "membership" in the club.

Once, *The Travelers' Club* presented a short clip showing a crowd gathered at one of the synagogues in the US. The whole episode lasted only for a few minutes, but in that time I noticed many happy faces among the members of the congregation. In contrast, their Soviet counterparts were not allowed to appear near any synagogue.

The image of American Jews freely attending synagogue was my first inkling that in the United States citizens were protected from discrimination and religious persecution, and it gave me something to hope for when deciding to leave my homeland. I was determined not to live in fear any longer. It was comforting and inspiring to think that America was built by immigrants who had all been stateless or displaced at some point.

One of my friends, Alex, went to the US on a business trip as a scientist. His visit occurred a few weeks before my multigenerational family was scheduled to depart the Soviet Union. The youngest was Olga Shapiro, my daughter. There was Vadim Shapiro, my then-husband; Neli Melman, my mother; Susan Shapiro, my mother-in-law; Peter Pershikov, Susan's husband (and Vadim's stepfather); and Berta Melman, my eighty-six-year-old grandmother.

Full of fear and uncertainty, I impatiently waited to talk to Alex after his return. I wanted to get his firsthand observations of how Soviet refugees were adjusting to a new life.

We met for dinner at his apartment. At first he made reassuring and comforting statements: "During my trip I met many wonderful Americans. They were very nice to me; even strangers tried to help when I couldn't find directions to some of my destinations. They said hello to me at the stores, in the elevators, or just on the street." This report contrasted with Soviet portrayals of Americans as disrespectful to foreigners.

Then I asked my burning question: "Did you meet any physicians who emigrated from the Soviet Union and were relicensed in the US? Was it difficult to find a job after they passed all the mandatory exams?"

Alex paused. A cloud of gloom seemed to descend over the dining table. "Well," he muttered, "I heard from a few people that former Soviet physicians who came to the US were unable to provide proof of their doctoral degrees in medicine. Consequently, they didn't get a license to practice medicine."

To earn the right to practice in the United States, foreign-trained doctors had to pass the first two parts of the United States Medical Licensing Examination, be certified by the Educational Commission for Foreign Trained Medical Graduates, enter a residency program, and pass the third licensing test. Another barrier for Soviet doctors was acquiring a mastery of English.

"What happened to all these doctors?" I asked.

My friend's answer startled me: "I met a few physicians who had practiced in Ukraine. They made several attempts to pass extremely complicated exams to become eligible for a residency program at one of the hospitals. This crucial step would have completed their re-training. These doctors failed the exams and never returned to their profession."

"What are they doing instead?" I asked. At this moment I was not thinking of those doctors; I was thinking of myself.

Alex's responses did not assuage my fears. He reported that "some of these doctors became taxi drivers. Others found jobs in sales." I noticed a touch of hesitation in his voice. "Those who could not find any job were out on the street."

"That's enough!" I raised my voice. "We are ready to leave in a few weeks and this can't be changed. My family has pulled through the bureaucratic deceptions of the Chernobyl disaster, decades of discrimination and persecution, and the open expression of anti-Semitism. I am ready to face new challenges and to overcome them. I believe that the Jewish community in the US will welcome and support us."

Following that discussion with Alex, I avoided anyone who might weaken my resolve.

CHAPTER 10

Citizen without a Country

KIEV, UKRAINE, USSR, JUNE 1989

My inner voice welled up, increasingly impatient: *Alla, wake up! Alla!*

It was like a frightening dream, yet I was awake. Having entered a dark tunnel of no hope, I felt physically lifeless and numb, yet I also experienced profound emotional pain. As I became fully conscious of the place, and my reason for being there, I winced. I thought of the many years of persecution that had brought me and my family to this point. Along with hundreds of thousands of other emigrants, we were leaving the Soviet Union as Jews, in search of a life that would be free of discrimination.

I leaned back and flinched as my shoulders touched hard concrete. I was the only occupant of a bare gray room. A lone dusty lightbulb hung from the ceiling. Suddenly, a voice barked through a piece of steel mesh that covered a small opening in the wall. Where was the face? A hairy arm reached through the opening toward me.

"Give me your passport and hurry up!" commanded the voice, which rasped with irritation.

I was thirty-five years old and had never seen an arm that could talk. I forced myself to return to reality, and I remembered my purpose for being in that creepy building: to surrender my Soviet citizenship. I struggled to remain calm.

Alla, get a grip on yourself! No more thoughts, no more feelings! Hand over your Soviet passport and leave this hostile place as quickly as possible. Detach, stay calm, my inner voice counseled. *Your passport is just paper in a pretty red cover embossed with golden letters. It says that you are Alla, a woman, born in Kiev, whose "nationality" is identified as "Jewish." You can remember this without your passport.*

The arm slithered away, clutching my passport, then returned, holding a crinkled piece of dingy paper, carelessly ripped from the newspaper of the Communist Party. On it was scribbled some words that seemed warped, as if they were melting.

Then a cry escaped from my soul. In that sound were all the losses, loneliness, and betrayals I was living with. Tears streamed down my cheeks and onto the paper, which read, "This document is given to a person who is not a citizen of any country."

My very essence—my life, my dreams, my roots—had been written off in one cruel sentence. I had no country. *Who welcomes a person who has been stripped of citizenship?* My mind roiled in a battle between darkness and light, and as the darkness began to prevail, I thought, *No! Alla, you must let go of who you were so that you can become who you dream of becoming. Let the sorrow transform into something larger, stronger, and full of light. That light will illuminate your path to the future.*

CHAPTER 11

Becoming Immigrants

S oon we would be leaving Kiev, seeking entry to the United States via the "Vienna-Rome pipeline." I told my family that we would be going through two phases as we transformed ourselves from Soviet citizens to immigrants. The essential first stage would be to give free rein to our imaginations, allowing cherished images and memories and flights of fantasy to soothe our souls. This short-lived phase would end when the creative juices ran dry—and when the time came to face reality. Then each family member would be jolted into the practical phase.

I nicknamed my family "The Magnificent Seven," after John Sturges's 1960 classic Western. This was a remake of a Japanese adventure movie, Akira Kurosawa's *The Seven Samurai*. In this inspiring story about a village of farmers who hired seven gunmen to prevent marauding bandits from stealing their crops, the gunmen taught the farmers to use courage and resourcefulness in self-defense. We would need those qualities on our journey.

My family members were opinionated, outspoken, and apparently possessed of great minds, though none of us thought alike. Our divergent ideas would have to give way to consensus when we had limited choices regarding shelter, food, personal hygiene, and the like. We would be forced to find solutions that would meet the needs of all four generations.

Yet, on the plane from Kiev, I could still embrace the imagination stage. I thought of Vienna, with its shining history of colorful characters like Wolfgang Mozart and Gustav Klimt. Mostly I thought of Johann Strauss, whose well-known compositions such as "Tales from the Vienna Woods" helped establish him as the "Waltz King." This waltz earned Strauss a place in music history. Composed in 1868, it reflected the history of the dance from its humble village origins to its adoption by Viennese high society.

Alas, I did have an unwelcome association with "Tales from the Vienna Woods." It was part of the soundtrack for a 1987 film, *Escape from Sobibor*, the story of a Nazi death camp during World War II. The extermination centers scattered throughout Eastern Poland had the sole purpose of killing as many Jews as possible as quickly as possible. In the movie, the music from "Vienna Woods" was played during every scene where trains crammed with Jews arrived at Sobibor. That music had been used to soothe, to allay fears, and to ensure the compliance of new arrivals to the camp.

My family and I had left the Soviet Union voluntarily, but the realization that ours was an exit with no return hit me hard. I contemplated the apparent finality of emigration: it meant never revisiting our birthplace. That thought made me long to pay respects to the family members laid to rest there. The silence of their graves would make me feel at peace with my decision. Then I pictured my family as a tree without roots and became more and more pessimistic as my former life receded and the plane soared through the miles.

FIG. 4. *Arrival,* a sculpture by my friend Eva Shankman showing people at the entrance to a concentration camp. *Photograph courtesy of the artist.*

As we deplaned in Vienna, we had our first unpleasant encounter with the realities of life as refugees. Along with almost two hundred other refugees leaving the plane with their one-way tickets, we anticipated a warm welcome. Instead, as we set foot into the crowded airport, a harsh voice with an unexpected accent told us to remain in place until further notice. The voice came from an Israeli man in a sombrero with a brim wide enough to cast a shadow over his face, neck, and shoulders. The first words in heavily accented Russian to emerge from beneath his hat were derisive: "Hey, you! Going to the US? Think you'll find happiness living on welfare there?" The man did his appalling best to dissuade us from our American destination, lamely hoping we would go instead to the Holy Land.

The newcomers were dumbstruck. An elderly man standing next to me started to tremble with outrage. My reflexive response froze on my lips. *But didn't you once come here also in search of happiness?*

Probably, the mocking sombrero man had found his new home and employment in Austria quite recently. His face remained invisible, and the only part of him that I could see were his short arms, which moved in different directions as he indicated where the passengers should go.

I later characterized my first hours and days in Vienna as a shock. As a physician, I didn't use this word lightly. The jolt that I experienced was like that induced by severe trauma or other life-threatening condition or disease. My mind spiraled downward in a final stage of distress, when physical disequilibrium begins to take a permanent toll on the body. Yet I was compelled to set aside a hurricane of thoughts and emotions, including sorrow and hopelessness.

Do all these people, who accepted a crumpled piece of paper declaring them to be stateless, who obeyed an arm pointing in a direction of "no return," deserve to be viewed as unwanted burdens? Are they doomed to become street-corner beggars, welfare-dependent recipients, delinquents, and criminals? Will hostility toward newcomers be their new reality?"

As we left the building, I tried to assuage my profound pain with humor. I forced a laugh at the billboard depicting Vienna International Airport as one that "creates the ideal environment for a relaxing holiday or business trip."

As I boarded the bus, I muttered, "Adios, sombrero man. I hope I never see you again."

CHAPTER 12

The Tale of the Wandering Jew

Affter the short journey from Kiev to Vienna, irreconcilable differences emerged amongst the members of our Magnificent Seven. To get through the challenges of our journey, we returned again to our imaginations.

Little Olga enjoyed exploring, and in the process, she picked up new words, temporary new friends, and many creative ideas. Olga and I once overheard a neighbor from the Vienna villa playing with her daughter. They called their amusement "Game of Situations," a playful distraction from reality. The mother would ask the child a question about a hypothetical situation. The little girl would picture it and respond. The neighbor's game inspired Olga and me to create our own version.

First, I painted a picture of Olga's upcoming sixth birthday party at an undisclosed location, since we didn't know where we would be when her birthday arrived. Olga would be sitting at the children's table surrounded by new friends and favorite desserts.

"One of your friends was not careful and dropped a piece of a cherry pie on the white tablecloth," I began. "Olga, who did it?"

My daughter knew exactly who committed this hypothetical blunder. She pleasantly surprised me with her answer: "Sorry, Mom, I did it."

A second round of the game began with the two of us lying on a beach in Italy. A young, handsome man approached and asked me a question that a nice Italian fellow would never dare ask: "Signora, how old are you?" I responded that I was twenty-five years old. Olga, forgetting that we were playing a game of make-believe, jumped off her chair and yelled, "Why are you lying, Mom?"

Olga's victory in the Game of Situations signaled a return to the reality of our wandering life. The process of packing, repacking, and unpacking was painful for me. For years after we settled in the US, I felt nauseated whenever I looked at suitcases in the basement.

When we were packing to move from Austria to Italy, I had a conversation with an imaginary friend I had created to keep me company. I pictured him as Italian because he would be familiar with refugees in Italy trying to move to the US, and he would express compassion for them.

"Have you ever heard of a wandering Italian?" I asked him. The Italian friend shook his head no. "Have you ever heard of a wandering Singaporean?" I continued. The look I got should have stopped my questioning. Yet I pressed on. "What about a wandering Jew?"

The friend replied without hesitation: "Of course! Wandering is a part of Jewish destiny; they have learned to survive homelessness, statelessness, and persecution."

"How does the saga end?" I asked.

"This story never ends," he answered.

I wasn't surprised when my friend reappeared and suggested a book entitled *The Wandering Jews*, by Joseph Roth (1894–1939). An

Austrian-Jewish journalist and novelist, Roth is known for his novels about Jewish life and for newspaper reporting from countries throughout Europe.

As a Jew and a well-known critic of Nazism, Roth had to leave Germany when Hitler came to power. On January 30, 1933, the day that Hitler seized control of Germany, Roth fled to Paris and never returned. *The Wandering Jews* recounts stories in which Jewish refugees seek shelter in cities and towns where they are always made unwelcome. Roth, who suffered from chronic alcoholism and anxiety, continued writing novels depicting the deep sense of homelessness of Jewish wanderers in Europe after World War I and the Russian Revolution. In 1926 Roth visited the Soviet Union, where he wrote *The Condition of the Jews in Soviet Russia*. Soviet Jews found themselves homeless and persecuted, with no option but to seek refuge outside their homeland. In 1939 Roth, at forty-four, died of tuberculosis in Paris, where he had lived since fleeing Hitler's Berlin in 1933.

Roth's close Jewish friend Stefan Zweig was a talented, prolific writer. He was Austrian and an outspoken liberal pacifist who came under pressure from his country's authoritarian regime. Zweig moved to England in 1934, and later traveled to Petropolis, Brazil. He mistakenly thought there was no better place for him. Roth and Zweig were compelled to wander because each country where they sought refuge rejected them or made them feel unwanted. This is the plight of the wandering Jew. Zweig's books were burned and banned in Germany. In 1942 in Petropolis, he and his wife, Lotte, committed suicide using barbiturates.[21]

At times during the long journey from the Soviet Union to the US, I feared that my family's voyage would never end. We spent months in Italy waiting for permission to enter the United States. *Is*

it just a troublesome situation, or a curse, to wander endlessly, depend-
ing on the odds of cities or countries being hostile or welcoming? Nevertheless, I refused to see myself as an eternally wandering Jew. I
never wanted to lose my sense of self again as I had been forced to do
when leaving the Soviet Union.

Long after the Magnificent Seven finally put down roots in Washington, DC, where a new generation of American citizens was born,
I marveled at the human capacity to resettle and build a better life,
and I thought often of the brave spirit of the wandering Jew.

One day my co-worker and friend Muriel brought me something
to brighten my afternoon. It was an elegant plant that she had carefully nurtured. I was deeply moved by this living gift, with its long,
trailing vines and green leaves with faint purple accents. "How lovely,
Muriel," I exclaimed. "What is it called?"

"This houseplant is called Wandering Jew, and it grows so easily
that even a baby can grow it," my friend replied. In this way Muriel
introduced me to the actual plant, which, like my family, spread and
grew strong roots.

CHAPTER 13

Prequel to the "Trans-Siberian" Express

There are times in our lives when we have to realize our past is precisely what it is, and we cannot change it. But we can change the story we tell ourselves about it, and by doing that, we can change the future.
—ELEANOR BROWN, *THE WEIRD SISTERS*[22]

From Vienna an overnight train took the family to Rome, a trip that seemed as prolonged as the eight-day ride from Beijing to Moscow depicted in the movie thriller *Trans-Siberian*. All night long a loud group of fellow émigrés in the adjacent cabin competed all too successfully with the general ruckus of the moving train.

Trans-Siberian was released in 2008, when my family was living in the US. The scenario for this thriller must have been based on stories heard on a journey similar to ours. During their train voyage, the American couple in the film meets a Russian police inspector who is trailing the killers of a drug dealer. The couple find themselves involved in attempts to smuggle narcotics, which were hidden inside "matryoshka," Russian nesting dolls.

Our rowdy neighbors seemed embroiled in something similarly illicit—or at least desperate. Through the carriage walls we could hear

FIG. 5. My three dear friends and fellow Soviet émigrées re-enact our experiences on the train as we fabricated stories to secure our immigration. From left to right are Irene Feldman, Julia Imas, and Slava Leykin. *Photograph, 2017, by Alla Shapiro.*

them plotting to enhance their prospects of obtaining refugee status with the American consulate in Rome. In 1989 the qualifying rules were so stringent that refugees thought their stories of persecution in the Soviet Union had to be even more extreme than they were.[23]

Inside the next-door car, packed with eight people, a story of deception and murder emerged. I overheard them talking about a family member who was presumed dead, but who was, in fact, traveling on our train. Repeatedly they mentioned "caskets" and also "matryoshka" —just like in the film! Their tortured fiction was intended to bring tears to the eyes of the American Consulate staff. I later learned that their story was a smashing success, and the entire family was granted refugee status.

CHAPTER 14

This Was No "Roman Holiday"

PAVONA, ITALY, JULY 1989

My family, along with tens of thousands of other immigrants, was affected by the US government's new policy to limit the number of Soviet Jews entering the country as political refugees. This group remained stuck in Italy as they awaited permission to move to the United States.

Our life in Italy was nothing like *Roman Holiday*, a romantic comedy filmed in 1953. In the movie, the heroine, named Ann, was played by Audrey Hepburn. Her character, the crown princess of an unspecified country, went on a widely publicized tour of several European capitals, including Rome. Humor, mystery, and romance infused her adventures. The movie ended with the heroine returning home, perhaps to continue with her royal responsibilities. In contrast, I came from a specific country, the USSR. Yet in my sole official document, I was listed as an unspecified, or stateless, person.

My family and I joined the inhabitants of Pavona, a small seaside town in central Italy where fewer than 14,000 Italians lived. The expanding population of former Soviet citizens stressed the town's

resources. Pavona had three schools, a library, and a few Roman cas-
tles. With its dusty, unpaved streets, it was the stark opposite of Kiev.
During our ten-day stay at Villa Maria, we were homesick. We missed
our friends in Kiev, and we wrote letters to them about the town and
our apartment.

Many of these friends were nervously awaiting emigration, and
they shared our letters with others eager to learn more about life
outside the Soviet Union. Some of our letters were read aloud at
small gatherings of friends, who imagined crossing the Soviet border
to Italy. But after hearing my candid descriptions of accommoda-
tions in Pavona, would-be refugees looked with greater appreciation
at their familiar, comparatively comfortable, apartments in Kiev. The
usual lack of running water in their apartments during the summer
months seemed a minor deprivation in contrast.

The room at Villa Maria was about ten feet by thirteen feet. My
family of seven was crammed into this small space designed for one or
two. We had an uninspiring view of barracks-style buildings outside
the window. My efforts to hoist the youngest or smallest family members to the top level of double bunk beds without a ladder were heroic.

The bathroom adjacent to the room looked like something exca-
vated from ancient Roman ruins. Despite its archaic appearance, the
toilet generated impressive water pressure while flushing. The stream
was so powerful that it sprayed me with much of the water from the
bowl, which left me feeling like the ancient Romans must have felt
after a trip to the nearby Caracalla Baths.

These public baths were built between AD 212 and 216, during
Emperor Caracalla's reign. The emperor employed an early kind of
political propaganda in building the baths so that the public would
like and remember him. Romans from every social class enjoyed

themselves in the impressive, exquisitely detailed building.[24] Their
pleasure in the soothing baths and lavish surroundings created a
sense of unity and elevated public opinion of Caracalla. *One day I
will come back as a tourist to this attraction,* I thought wistfully.

Strolling along the barracks of Villa Maria on an unpaved road,
we came to a dining room, where all the temporary residents of
Pavona met for meals: generous servings of spaghetti topped with
butter for breakfast; spaghetti with hard boiled eggs for lunch; and
spaghetti, again, with tomato sauce for dinner. Strangers became
friends on the main street of Pavona, where they exchanged often-as-
tounding stories from the past and concerns about the future. Sharing these stories served as a kind of rehearsal for those awaiting their
immigration interview at the American Consulate.

Many in the Pavona group told life stories that were devastating
and sad. For instance, Jacob, a frail seventy-year-old man who walked
with a stoop, was a decorated World War II veteran who in 1945 had
fought against German forces to liberate Vienna. In 1944 he entered
the Majdanek camp in Poland, where he released thousands of concentration camp prisoners and brought them to freedom. Without any
ambitions for building his own life in America, Jacob was one of the
immigrants who could not imagine life without their families and was
simply following the younger generations. Finding himself a voluntary
prisoner in a bleak Pavona refugee camp was for him tragically ironic.
His dark sense of humor failed to mask his depression. Over and over
he said, "Days spent in Pavona seem to be as bright as Alaska in
December." This was his last testimony, for Jacob died after four months
in Italy, his final resting place one of default, not of choice.

Freedom of choice had little meaning for many other elderly
Soviet Jewish immigrants who, like Jacob, did not choose refugee

transit shelters as the final stop for their life's journey. They died without making the connection between freedom and choice.

Another man in the group, Peter, was a brilliant forty-year-old scientist from Moscow who had to leave his authoritarian country to evade discrimination. While living in Moscow he had devoted his life and research to constructing large surface vessels to carry anti-submarine helicopters. After completing his doctoral dissertation, he successfully launched helicopters from a vessel. On that basis he hoped for acceptance by the elite Soviet scientific society. But Peter's Moscow superior told him that his obviously Jewish last name precluded him from professional involvement in the scientific project he had developed. When Peter's colleagues—all with Russian last names—heard about this, they made him a target of offensive jokes. Peter resigned. He explained to his wife and twelve-year-old daughter that the career he had hoped for was not to be. The family packed for the US and soon found themselves in Pavona, awaiting an interview at the American Consulate in Rome.

Shortly thereafter, Peter received a letter denying his request for entry to the US. People who had been denied access to their immigration country of choice were labeled "refuseniks." More than ten thousand such refuseniks were stuck in Italy. Devastated, Peter fell into a deep depression and had hallucinations of Russian helicopters launched from vessels in the Pavona harbor. He took a final glimpse at the shore and, dressed only in underwear, stepped into a small fishing boat and disappeared. For a time, Peter's wife and daughter watched a boat with an old man who resembled Peter floating on the water near Pavona. Some friends silently accompanied the grieving pair to the shore. Peter was never seen again.

Peter's departure shocked me and gave me pause. If this could happen to one as strong and bright as Peter, could instability born of despair spread among refugees of Pavona, including my own relatives?

My family, along with many others, continued our uncertain existence in Italy for months as we hoped and waited for visas. Eventually, things would change for the better.

When we arrived in Vienna in June 1989, we could choose to go to Israel or the United States. Most of us chose the latter (although Israel wanted us to go there) and were sent to Italy to apply for US refugee status at the American Consulate in Rome. After that we thought we would be permitted to immigrate to the US.

Previously, Jews from the Soviet Union were *presumed* to be political refugees and did not have to provide compelling evidence that they had been persecuted. Now we did have to tell our stories of persecution. Even so, within about a week after our arrival in Italy, our applications were rejected. We decided to stay and wait for some resolution.

The problem was that the US did not anticipate so many refugees and did not have the funds to support them all. Therefore, the US made it more difficult for immigrants to qualify for refugee status. As the American Embassy rejected an increasing number of visa applications from Soviet Jews, the Jewish émigré communities in Ladispoli and Santa Marinella grew. In July 1989 an estimated 16,000 Jewish refugees were stalled in Italy, and by the end of that year there were 40,000.

Meanwhile, leaders of the American Jewish community protested their government's rejection of Soviet Jews as refugees and accused consular officials of discrimination. Responding to pressure from the American Jewish Community, on November 21, 1989, Congress passed the Lautenberg Amendment. Under this amendment, every Soviet Jewish émigré potentially could be considered for refugee status. However, of some 40,000 Jewish refugees in 1989, the US government would only fund 32,000. The American Jewish community had to fund the placement of the remaining 8,000.[25] In this way America opened its gates to everyone in Italy who qualified for refugee status.

In December 1989, my family flew from Rome to Washington, DC.

CHAPTER 15

Live Hard, Sell Hard

The Americana Flea Market in Rome

SANTA MARINELLA, ITALY, AUGUST 1989

After ten days in Pavona, our Magnificent Seven spent several months in Santa Marinella, a picturesque town about thirty-six miles northwest of Rome in the Italian region of Lazio. The place is famous for its "Wheels of Immigration"—a pretzel-like snack that was enjoyed by Russian Jewish immigrants who temporarily settled there in the late 1980s on their way to the United States or some other destination, such as Canada or Australia. Santa Marinella was also regarded as a favorable location from which Soviet refugees could make their way to the famous flea market, Americana, which was halfway to Rome from there.

During the brutally hot summer of 1989, my family stayed in a modest three-bedroom apartment in a big villa. The apartment, which was tiny despite the number of so-called "bedrooms," looked like a train with three cars. The second and third cars did not have windows, and the first and second cars lacked doors. One hallmark of this architectural design was lack of privacy: many obviously private conversations were unintentionally overheard.

The term "economic dependence" frequently cropped up in the conversations of our stateless group. It was a frightening term for those confronted with a strange language and an unfamiliar culture. To reduce their own economic dependence, people who inhabited the refugee camps across Italy tried desperately to sell anything they could—primarily Soviet goods they had brought with them—to support themselves beyond mere survival. The ninety dollars that each person was given when leaving the Soviet Union was not nearly enough. Sometimes, refugees waited a few months for permission to move to the US from Italy.

I had to learn to sell, even though the idea of it filled me with fear and shame. I had grown up during a time in the Soviet Union when people in merchandising were considered thieves who thrived with impunity in a criminal enterprise. In the late 1980s these thieves (to whom the law did not apply) controlled the retail trade and directed the distribution of goods. Supplies of almost all merchandise in the Soviet Union was limited. People who worked in the stores oversaw "free trade," a twisted version of supply and demand. Vendors were free to distribute goods that were in the store, at their discretion, to family, friends, and, especially, "business friends," those who worked in the different branches of the retail trade.

There was also a market for the exchange of goods between "partners in crime." A supply intended for the abovementioned individuals and groups was kept in a store's back rooms. I knew that there was no system of fair trade in the country, and everyone who benefitted from such exchanges was branded a thief by decent Soviet people. Only after living in the US did I conclude that, if good people are put in bad systems, you get bad results.

Yet things were not so simple when I was refining my sales skills at the Americana flea market. No matter how hard I tried, I was unable to overcome my reticence. I could not even develop a sales pitch. One day I noticed a potential customer who seemed interested in something I was selling: an unusual item, a telescope, which was taking up most of the area that I had reserved at 4:00 a.m. that day. The machine was powerful enough to detect the details of craters on the moon. As a curious gentleman hastened his step toward my spot, I deemed the sale a foregone conclusion. This was my moment to explain that the telescope was made in a factory taken by the Soviets from the Germans after the war, to advertise its German precision and quality, and to demonstrate its powers of magnification.

Instead, rational and pragmatic considerations disappeared from my mind. I abruptly turned and started running away from the customer. I had never run so fast, and had never felt so relieved. The telescope had been packed up by Olga's dad, who witnessed my capitulation in disbelief. Months later, before leaving Italy, I sent the telescope as a piece of luggage, and it reached New York City before my family arrived in Washington. After it lost its sentimental significance for me, I sold it online in the US.

A five-pointed red-star pin with a photograph of a young, curly-haired Lenin was an unexpected hit in the Americana market. This pin was given to all schoolchildren in the Soviet Union. At first, this unique item did not sell, as neither Italians nor Americans who visited the popular flea market were interested in Lenin. Those who gambled on what they thought would be a surefire sale were disappointed. But failure was not an option for those stateless souls trying to survive, and desperation became the mother of invention.

FIG. 6. In the center of this star-shaped pin, given to all schoolchildren in the Soviet Union, is an image of Vladimir Lenin as a child. The pin was in high demand in 1989 at the Americana market in Italy after a fellow Soviet refugee claimed that the image was of a famous soccer player, Alexander Zavarov. *Photograph by Alla Shapiro.*

A good friend of mine from Kiev days, Leonid, saw an opportunity to promote sales by inventing a backstory that would entice people to buy the pin. With fanfare, Leonid dangled the shiny star around for all to see, singing the praises of "young Zavarov," a famous soccer player of the 1980s from Ukraine, whose curly blond hair and boyish head resembled the 1870s image of Lenin as a little boy. Leonid's sales pitch rang out: "Prego, signoras and signors, don't miss this exceptional opportunity. Make this valuable piece of memorabilia yours!"

Customers flocked to Leonid. As he clinched each sale, he beamed a contagious smile and thanked the buyer. Too soon, demand exceeded inventory. Leonid promised to put disappointed buyers on a (fictitious) waiting list, and he pocketed the hope that came with his flea market success.

Who was this Alexander Zavarov who had dramatically boosted sales of a pin sporting young Lenin's face set in a red star? The only resemblance between the Zavarov and Lenin images was the hair. Zavarov was known as one of the most talented soccer players of his time. In 1986 he was named the best soccer player in the USSR and the sixth best football player in Europe. When the walls of Soviet power fell, a high transfer fee sent Alexander Zavarov from the Ukrainian team Dynamo Kiev to the Italian team Juventus. In 1988 and 1990 Juventus won the Coppa Italia (Italy Cup).[26] Young Lenin/Zavarov smiled bravely on the pin.

What became of Alexander Zavarov? During Ukraine's 2014 civil war, the nation's most respected citizens, including the coaches and the soccer team, were recruited to fight. Zavarov, the coach for Ukraine's national team at the time, was not exempt. He was one of eighty-nine men from the Soccer Federation of Ukraine who was ordered to fight.[27] However, he refused to participate in Ukraine's civil war, and with his resistance, the former soccer star acquired an unofficial name—refusenik. He collaborated with other protesters who opposed the Russian military intervention in the Ukraine in 2014. Customarily, if a person refuses to go into the army, he goes to jail. Zavarov escaped that fate, though the Soccer Federation of Ukraine did not extend Assistant Coach Zavarov's contract.

The famous soccer player represented a new generation of refuse-niks—not like those Soviet citizens, especially Jews, who were refused permission to emigrate as early as the 1970s. In the late 1980s, when the unexpected tide of Soviet Jews seeking to emigrate overwhelmed US cities, the United States closed off immigration routes sooner than expected. With this abrupt change in policy, the Magnificent Seven became Italian refuseniks.

My daughter, Olga, and many other former Soviet school boys and girls, are now adults living in America. They may not remember their trips to the flea market or their parents' chants: "Long live young Zavarov!" and "Farewell Comrade Lenin!" For the adults, however, selling in the Americana market was a rite of passage to the capitalist West!

CHAPTER 16

The Pretty Woman's Guide to Hitchhiking

Even though the Communist Party controlled the release and viewing of foreign movies and television shows, under the KGB's ever-watchful eye, *La Piovra* (The Octopus), a wildly popular series about the Italian Mafia, aired in the Soviet Union during the late 1980s. Italian actor Michele Placido starred as Police Inspector Corrado Cattani, and he investigated Mafia crimes. All my girlfriends and I were madly in love with Michele Placido, who was as charming as he was handsome. We found out as much as we could about the actor and his wife, actress Simonetta Stefanelli, best known as Michael Corleone's Sicilian first wife in *The Godfather*.

Women fantasized about Michele divorcing his wife and falling madly in love with them. My friends, like Simonetta Stefanelli, were in their forties (or, like me, even younger) and so felt that they still had a chance with him. They dreamed that he was the sort of man who called his mother-in-law "Cara Mia Mamma"—my beloved mother—a fantasy that brought sentimental tears to their eyes. I saw in Placido a most desirable combination: masculine, confident, elegant, powerful, and drenched in sex appeal. Silky smooth and sophisticated, he seemed capable of handling any situation.

Animated, adoring discussions followed each episode. My girl-friends imagined that he would become police inspector in Ukraine, bringing ruthless criminals to justice and improving the quality of life in the Soviet Union. However, the series ended abruptly with Cattani's murder. Fans were shocked. A friend of mine called, sobbing, "Is this really The End?"

Escapist flights of fancy were common among Soviet citizens. We traded the gray reality of day-to-day life for a few hours of watching foreign movies and television. During the months in Santa Marinella, I frequently recalled Italian movies and shows I'd seen, like *La Piovra*. Thus, I could escape through the door of my imagination while awaiting the next leg of our journey.

Santa Marinella was the setting of a prominent movie star's love affair. Ingrid Bergman, among the greatest actresses of her generation and one of my favorites, once lived in a villa in Santa Marinella. The Swedish star wrote a letter to Italian producer Roberto Rossellini, who, like Bergman, was at the top of his career. It read:

"Dear Mr. Rossellini, I saw your films *Open City* and *Paisan*, and enjoyed them very much. If you need a Swedish actress who speaks English very well, who has not forgotten her German, who is not very understandable in French, and who in Italian knows only 'ti amo,' I am ready to come and make a film with you."[28] The letter ignited one of the most passionate love affairs in film history. I thought that the letter was charming and seductive.

Unfortunately, there was no heartthrob to whom I could write a letter. I couldn't even say that I was "a physician who speaks English very well, who has not forgotten her German, and who is not very understandable in French." Refugees caught lying would have no chance of making it to America.

I shook my head, reluctantly returning to reality after such pleasant reveries. I faced the fact that I was a refusenik in Italy. Refuseniks originally were citizens of the Soviet Union who were denied permission to emigrate. The word later came to include refugees who had left the Soviet Union and were stalled in Italy awaiting government approval to emigrate to the US.

This transient group received extra boxes of spaghetti, Italy's beloved pantry staple. My family members regularly picked up the spaghetti rations, standing in line week after week for the linear pasta. I loathed the chore and developed a deep resentment of the entire pasta industry. Therefore, I resorted to escaping through my mind. I recalled learning, from a book I had read as a child, about pasta shops that had appeared in Italy since the twelfth century. I visualized eighteenth-century English aristocrats on a grand tour across Italian cities, where pasta hung to dry—in the streets, on balconies, and on rooftops. *Why is the history of pasta as tangled as spaghetti on a plate?* I wondered. *Was it Marco Polo who introduced this product to Italy? Of course, not. Marco was a great explorer and merchant who came to the world with more serious intentions. He brought back from China gunpowder, fireworks, silk, and jewels. His restless spirit would not agree with the romantic claims related to him about something as boring as pasta.* My imagination turned to nineteenth-century Neapolitan street vendors, bowls of grated Romano cheese beside them, selling spaghetti from stalls with charcoal-fired stoves. They held long strands high above their faces then dropped them into their mouths. Delighted customers mimicked the ritual.

It was time for me to awake from my daydream and get the spaghetti ration, stored at a rundown building on the outskirts of town. To make the errand more enjoyable, I decided to bring Olga with me to the pasta warehouse, which was several miles from the family's villa apartment, a distance too difficult for a six-year-old to walk. So, I engaged in a ruse that I called the "pretty Russian woman," a sequence of steps that I had seen Soviet women take to get from point A to point B in Italy. Born of the immigration experience, the plan employed humor and deception.

Having little money, refugees found that a family trip to the local grocery store on a city bus was comparable in cost to an expensive limo ride to a luxury resort. Hitchhiking seemed a solution. An unwritten but widely known "Hitchhikers' Guide" circulated among the refugees. The "manual" instructed that the proper combination of hitchhikers was essential for success: young mothers—preferably blondes—and their daughters made a perfect combination. Second best was a young woman and her younger sister. Great-grand-mothers, grandmothers, and their sisters were the lamest ponies in the race. The recommended "waiting area" for men in a family of hitchhikers was near trees or bushes, where they should wait unno-ticed until after a ride was secured. Ditches in the road were a strate-gic plus for hitchhikers because they forced drivers to slow down. A young Russian mother with her child, looking desperate and waving her arm in the desired direction, completed the no-fail marketing scheme.

Unsuspecting drivers would stop, open the door, and utter an inviting, "Prego, signora." Once all were seated, signora would bestow a charming smile and softly say, "Bella Italia!" as she motioned toward her destination. I used this technique, hoping to avoid a long wait with Olga on that steamy day. A car approached through the dust on the horizon. I waved and, right on cue, the driver stopped his car, opened the door, and politely said, "Prego, signora."

I put Olga in the back seat and got in the front next to the driver. "Thank you," I said, staring straight ahead. Not having the spare money to take a bus, I always felt ashamed of hitchhiking, and did not look at the driver or talk to him. The first few minutes passed in silence. Then the driver asked, "Are you Russian?" I nodded, but quickly admonished myself: *This is not right—I should at least be polite.* The man was doing us a favor and not facing him when I spoke broke my code of etiquette. I turned toward the driver and froze: beside me in the driver's seat was the legendary Michele Placido, alive and well, looking at me with his irresistible smile. I blushed, my heart rate hitting a record high. "The End" certainly hadn't happened in Kiev—this instead was the ultimate Grand Finale!

Stuttering with emotion, I mixed Russian and English into a sort of "Russ-glish." I gushed tongue twisters of admiration over Michele Placido's acting skills, his abundant popularity in my homeland, and his dashing portrayal of a Mafia-fighting police officer. The star seemed to understand it all. Way too soon for my liking, we reached the storehouse. At that moment I hated the macaroni place more than ever, this time for being too close to home. Placido opened the front door and cheered me with his smile and warm wishes.

"Grazie mille," I grinned ecstatically. "Arrivederci, Inspector Cattani!"

CHAPTER 17

Global Events Unite Us

Aﬁter six months our Magniﬁcent Seven were granted their long-awaited visas, and we left Italy for the United States to pursue the American dream. On the long ﬂight from Rome to Washington, DC, I reviewed for the umpteenth time everything I had left behind in Kiev.

Landing in Washington, the seat of American government, made me think of two unforgettable events: the Cuban Missile Crisis and the assassination of President John F. Kennedy. Regarding the former, on October 22, 1962, the president delivered a televised speech of unprecedented gravity. He announced that US spy planes had detected the Soviet military installing nuclear missiles at sites in Cuba, a mere ninety miles from the Florida coast. These sites—under construction but near completion—housed projectiles capable of striking the United States, including the nation's capital.

Kennedy ordered a naval quarantine, or blockade, of Cuba to prevent Soviet ships from transporting additional offensive weapons to the island. He said that the United States would not tolerate the existence of the sites currently in place and demanded that Cuba dismantle the bases and remove the missiles. Over the next six days, the crisis escalated as the world teetered on the brink of a nuclear war between the two superpowers.[29]

Our elementary school teacher in Kiev delivered this horrifying news to my class of eight-year-old children. Schools across the Soviet Union closed, and students were sent home to be with their families. I was not allowed to walk home by myself and had to wait for my grandmother Berta to fetch me. When Grandma arrived, I was so afraid that the war was about to start that I burst into tears of relief when she appeared to escort me to safety.

By the third grade, I had seen more World War II movies than cartoons. Many of the movies included documentary footage of bombings of hospitals, which were frequently hit during German aviation raids. Civilian casualties, including doctors, were found in the areas of the strikes.[30] Scenes of the bodies of doctors and nurses remained starkly vivid in my memory because my mother was a doctor. Overwhelmed by such images and by fears of nuclear war, I was inconsolable.

Schoolchildren in the Soviet Union were kept at home while the USSR remained on high alert. The country was ready to strike the US if it showed what Soviet leaders viewed as aggression. But on October 28, 1962, Nikita Khrushchev, first secretary of the Communist Party of the Soviet Union, announced that the Soviet government would dismantle and remove all offensive Soviet weapons in Cuba.[31]

In a message broadcast on Radio Moscow, the USSR confirmed that it would proceed with this solution, which had been secretly proposed by the Americans the day before. By the afternoon, Soviet technicians had already begun dismantling the missile sites, averting nuclear war. The Cuban Missile Crisis was, effectively, over. On November 21 Kennedy called off the blockade, and by the end of the year all offensive missiles had left Cuba.[32]

Many years later the events and emotions experienced by American and Soviet children alike on opposite sides of the Cold War remain vivid. In both countries my generation prepared for the worst, learning to hide under school desks in case of nuclear attack from the enemy.

The airline stewardess interrupted my thoughts to announce our imminent approach to Washington. As we prepared to land, we watched a carpet of myriad lights become a glittering city of white marble monuments and large buildings. "I have never seen so many lights," I whispered in Olga's ear, as she tried to balance her motion sickness with delight in the spectacle.

Our family deplaned and proceeded to the US Customs checkpoint. The officer looked at my paper and smiled. "Welcome home," he said as he glanced at my papers again, and casually added, "Alla."

"Next, next, next . . ." The officer continued greeting others in this warm and hospitable manner. I sighed with relief, remembering the hostility of the sombrero man in Vienna.

What a wonderful difference it makes to be welcomed home by a perfect stranger in uniform!

Two members of Congregation Beth El of Bethesda, Maryland, met my family at the airport. The Jewish community of Greater Washington opened their arms to embrace us, and showered us with encouragement and support. Many of their members helped us through an extremely stressful time adapting to a new life. They said that we were their "adopted family."

FIG. 7. Berta and Olga are featured in this 1990 *Washington Jewish Week* article about Greater Washington's efforts to resettle a large influx of Soviet Jewish refugees.

Not long after my family settled in a small townhouse rental in the suburbs of Washington, we were invited to the Friday service and Shabbat dinner at Beth El with a few hundred other "family" members. The Soviet Jewry Committee, a newly established team at the synagogue, helped us navigate these new experiences.

One member of the congregation, Sonya, a polite and caring person, picked us up from home. When she entered our house, each of us in broken English tried to express gratitude to her for taking us to the synagogue and for being attentive and kind. Sonya listened patiently to a choir of six voices. When this was over, she said, "Don't thank me, please. I am happy that I am picking you up, and not the

Pulling out the stops for Soviet Jews

By Jon Greene
WJW Staff Writer

From Baku to Bethesda, Kiev to Kalorama and Moscow to Manassas, Soviet Jews are on their way.

The unprecedented wave of Soviet Jews coming to the United States and Israel has sent community groups into action to resettle the newcomers. In Washington, the ninth largest U.S. resettlement center, a $3.5 million community aid package has been established to bring as many as 600 Soviet Jews into mainstream American Jewish society.

"We see it as a total effort," said Phil Margolius, chairman of the community resettlement committee of the United Jewish Appeal Federation (UJAF). "We don't want them to plop themselves down here and get lost."

The federal government offers about $900 in resettlement assistance for each Soviet Jew granted refugee status, according to UJAF estimates. On top of that, the UJAF funds about $3200 per Soviet Jews, but the majority have not given up yet.

At Congregation Beth El in Bethesda, synagogue members faced the frustrating prospect of trying to get its new Soviet members involved in religious services without Russian prayerbooks.

"If you tell people to come to services, they won't understand them," said Debra Friedmann, chairperson of the synagogue's Soviet Jewry committee.

So Friedmann and others located a supply of Russian prayerbooks published in New Jersey. With a dozen books now on hand, the synagogue can actively involve its new members and reduce their level of frustration.

One of the most difficult transitions for newly arrived Soviet Jews involves finding employment. Many of the newcomer who hold prominent positions in skilled technical fields such as computer programming or engineering can fit in well with Washington's job market, but most cannot find work at the same status level they once held.

"One of the problems is the

'I want to give a Russian prayer book to all our new friends,' says Debra Friedmann, top left, Soviet Jewry Committee chairman at Temple Beth El in Bethesda as her son Joseph, 6, reads with Olga Shoshin, 6, and her...

FIG. 8. This 1990 *Washington Jewish Week* article reports on concerted local efforts to resettle newcomers from the Soviet Union. Pictured from left to right are Debra Friedman, her son Joseph, Olga, and myself. We are reading a Russian prayer book that these Temple Beth El members gave to us.

other way around. I cannot even imagine how I would feel if I were you. So, don't thank me."

At dinner, following the service at Beth El, one of the committee members asked if any of us newly arrived Soviet immigrants would like to say a few words to the congregation. At that time, I could not find enough English words in my vocabulary to express my immense gratitude to those who welcomed us to America, and who continued to help us to build our new lives. Our six-year-old daughter, Olga, came to my rescue.

"Mom," she whispered into my ear, "do you remember the poem that I wrote about America when we were living in Italy before we came here?"

"Sure, go ahead, Olga, recite your poem. This is a good time and a good place for it."

As parents, we had tried to build Olga's confidence since she was a baby. Our daughter had also independently learned some ways to increase her own self-assurance. She stepped forward and proudly presented her debut poem:

America, America, I love you soooo much,

But life is soooo unfair,

Since I can't see you, or touch.

I kept my head down, hesitating to look around. A few seconds later the congregation burst into applause. When I gazed at the crowd in the reception hall, I felt as if they were my family.

Olga was already at the dessert table, but it was high for her and she could not reach the surface. She looked around, her eyes asking for help. A few members of the synagogue rushed to serve this "celebrity." Olga wasted no time in taking advantage of the situation, and while I was busy answering questions about her poetry, she went on to her second slice of cake and was ready to start her pastry "marathon."

I faced many questions from my new extended family.

"Why did Olga write this poem? What prompted her to create it when you were in Italy? Did she know anything about the United States before you arrived here?"

This was my first interview on US soil, and I did not want to bungle it. During Olga's short presentation I recalled the circumstances that were the source of my daughter's inspiration. Vivid images reemerged of our stateless existence over the last six months.

We were stuck for so long in Santa Marinella, Italy, in 1989 that the communist deputy mayor of Ladispoli, in the suburbs of Rome, lamented, "People are beginning to ask, 'Are we losing our identity?' It is time to say, 'Enough.'" On one wall, vandals painted a swastika and the slogan, "Russians Go Home."[33]

During the long days of waiting for permission to leave, kids of all ages were infused by their families with the hope that one day they would get on the plane (widely coded as "transport") that would take them to America. Day after day, plane after plane, came and left. Many families received their visas, but our Magnificent Seven still remained on standby. Olga's experience of our "transport situation" was what inspired her first poem.

Many of the refugees initially received a letter rejecting their request to enter the US, but they still remained hopeful. In the interim, children created a new game called "Where Is My Transport?" Eventually, the families who had been refuseniks were permitted to leave Italy.

I shared this story with the members of Beth El, who listened attentively to every detail. I could feel their warmth and support. I shared our daughter's viewpoint: "America, America, I love you soooo much!"

CHAPTER 18

Barbie Also Wears a Stethoscope

From the moment I first laid eyes on a Barbie doll in a small shop in Italy, I was fascinated by the iconic, shapely, and oh-so-American doll, who seemed the embodiment of the American dream of beauty and confidence. This Barbie's near-perfection in my eyes was sealed by a tiny, plastic, electric blue stethoscope around her neck: this doll was a doctor like me! Right then and there, *my own dream,* my *American* dream, formed clearly in my mind.

As we stepped into the shop near the bus stop, Olga was whining to me that the day was too hot and the bus had been too crowded. Suddenly, the six-year-old was transfixed by the sight of Barbie Doctor. Mother and daughter joined the legions of girls, planet wide, who were enchanted by the plastic goddess.

"I will try hard very very hard and I will buy a Barbie Doctor for you and *me,*" I whispered to Olga.

My later mission to find a Barbie Doctor in the US proved fruitless, despite endless searches. Toy store shelves bulged with an array of Barbies, from Barbie Firefighter to Barbie Princess of Ancient Mexico. Barbies came dressed as aerobics instructors, briefcase-carrying executives, and even a World Cup Soccer Barbie. My expectations went up a notch after I found a Barbie Nurse, but the salesperson said, "Barbie Doctor is not sold in the US." He offered the lame suggestion that I buy Barbie Nurse and simply remove her white cap. So, for a time the search for Barbie Doctor ended.

Two years after seeing Barbie Doctor in the Italian shop, I earned a pediatric residency at Georgetown University Hospital in Washington, DC. I wore a cherished electric blue stethoscope that my longtime friend Julia had given me at my farewell party before I left

FIG. 9. "I will get what I want." My daughter, Olga, in 1990. She did get what she wanted, including a Barbie Doctor doll, children of her own, and a career as a teacher of children for whom English is a second language. *Photograph by Vadim Shapiro.*

Kiev. Julia had used all her family connections to find this made-in-Japan stethoscope, which I saw as an enduring symbol of my healing profession. I loved its vivid blue color, a shade reminiscent of lightning, ionized air glows, and electrical discharges.

Many goods from around the world, including those made in Japan, were nearly impossible to obtain. I placed extraordinary value on Julia's gift, a thoughtful gesture of professional trust in me and a wish for fulfillment of my hopes and dreams in the US. After my family settled in Washington, I was surprised to find at our local drug store an abundant supply of stethoscopes in various colors. I smiled at the surety that I would never trade my beloved electric blue medical instrument for any other.

On a balmy spring day in Washington, my American friend Stella shared her excitement over a new boyfriend. He was caring and sensitive, Stella said, and possessed a charming, classically Italian temperament. He was Sicilian and his accent enchanted her. I cautioned my friend that the Mafia also came from Sicily.

Stella encouraged me: "Do go on," she said.

I sighed dramatically and continued. "In 1282 during the French invasion of Sicily, the saying was born: Morte Alla Francia Italia Anela—MAFIA, meaning Death to the French is Italy's Cry."

"Don't you know anything else about Italy other than organized crime and secret societies?" retorted Stella.

"Sure, I do," I said. "Italy was the first place where I saw Barbie dolls dressed as doctors for sale in a store. Olga and I both fell in love with her, but I didn't have the money then to buy Barbie Doctor. I have searched endlessly for one of these dolls in the US, but I am told they don't exist here." Stella didn't seem to be impressed with my remarks.

The summer passed in a whirlwind of rotations, rounds, and exhausting night calls at the hospital, leaving me little time to think about anything else. I looked forward to November, when I could break for Thanksgiving, my favorite American holiday. I counted the many blessings that my family had received during three years in our new homeland. Yes, I still missed my neighbors in Kiev, whose doors were always open in case Olga stopped in for dinner, to watch TV, or just to play. I mused that neighbors in Kiev dropped by without the formality of an invitation. US friends and neighbors were more reserved and wanted visitation plans to be made well in advance.

The doorbell interrupted my thoughts. The mailman waved a greeting and pointed to a package he had left on the front stoop. I scooped up the package, glancing for a return address to see who had sent it. Not seeing one, I imagined a secret admirer. I opened the parcel, then looked in disbelief at the piercing blue eyes that stared from the velvet-lined box. Doctor Barbie smiled at me in perfect beauty, her long blonde hair falling around her shoulders.

My fascination grew when I saw a tiny baby doll in Barbie's arms. Like me, Barbie was a pediatrician. I delighted in the bright blue stethoscope dangling around her neck. That universally used instrument was invented by Dr. Rene Theophile Hyacinthe Laënnec, a French physician. The idea for his invention came when he watched two children sending signals to each other using a long piece of solid wood and a pin.[34]

I gingerly placed the stethoscope on the baby doll's chest and could not believe my ears: I heard rapid heartbeats through the stethoscope's miniature plastic tubes. I quickly thought of Stella as the prime anonymous sender-suspect. In just a few seconds on the phone, Stella confirmed that she and her Sicilian friend had arranged the delivery of Barbie Doctor from Italy to our house in Maryland. I expressed deep gratitude for their thoughtful gift.

Today, my pediatrician Barbie is thirty years old and still cradles the baby. Their home is a wide window sill in my office. There is a small change though: the baby's heart no longer beats audibly through the bright blue stethoscope. The battery couldn't keep the baby's heart beating that long. Or, maybe, the tiny heart just got tired of the fast rhythm of American life?

FIG. 10. Barbie also is a doctor. My daughter and I searched for a Barbie Doctor doll in America after seeing one in Italy. We finally received one as a gift. *Photograph by Alla Shapiro.*

CHAPTER 19

My Medical Residency, Take Two

The doctor is from New York!

—SUSAN, A SIX-YEAR-OLD PATIENT,
GEORGETOWN UNIVERSITY HOSPITAL, JUNE 1994

W hat it feels like to become a doctor for the *second* time has rarely been described.

Medical credentials from other countries, including the Soviet Union, were not accepted in the US, and my physician colleagues and I traveled uncharted territory on the path to recertification of our medical diplomas. The law applying to foreign medical graduates who intend to practice medicine in the US is strict. Regardless of former affiliations—ranging from practicing in walk-in clinics to professorships at large academic clinical centers—each foreign graduate was, and still is, required to pass three extremely rigorous exams before entering a medical residency program in the US. The exams cover knowledge of the preclinical and clinical science taught during four years of intense, full-time studies at medical schools in the US. Although I and other doctors from the former USSR had already taken the Hippocratic Oath upon graduation from medical school, we took it a second time:

> I swear by Apollo Healer, by Asclepius, by Hygeia, by Pana-
> cea, and by all the gods and goddesses . . . that I will carry out,
> according to my ability and judgment, this oath. . . . I will
> benefit my patients according to my greatest ability and I will
> do no harm or injustice to them. Neither will I administer a
> poison to anybody when asked to do so, nor will I suggest
> such a course. . . .

Through this rite of passage, we crossed the line between "I was a doctor" and "I am becoming a doctor again."

Years earlier, I had completed a pediatric residency in Kiev and a fellowship in pediatric hematology. I received a PhD degree in hematology and earned an assistant professorship in pediatrics at the medical school in Kiev. I worked hard to integrate my twin specialties and to become the best "double doctor" ever.

Now, mastery of English was my top priority. Conversation, debate, deliberation, and even small talk counted. Also important was the ability to clearly express myself orally and in writing. I had to master ordinary but nuanced aspects of communication, especially those conversations that involved emotional exchanges and medical instructions. I also paid careful attention to punctuation. Having come from the "ice age" of technology in the USSR, my second priority was to demonstrate familiarity with modern technology. For example, in America, cardiac monitors were wall mounted, precluding the need to manually measure patients' heart beats.

After passing recertification exams, my next challenge was to earn a place in the program that matched qualified residents with a three-year pediatric residency program. I interviewed at my pre-ferred match, Georgetown University Hospital (GUH) Pediatric Residency Program, and was accepted.

During my interview at GUH, I met a group of pediatric resi-dents who had just completed their first year of residency. They said that they worked miserable hours, with frequent thirty-six-hour shifts, yet they were among the nicest, happiest people I had ever met. These residents seemed to love their work and the children who were their patients. I listened in amazement to their stories of long, grueling hours on call with no sleep, and marveled at their easy laughter, cheerfulness, and affection for their colleagues.

On my first day of residency on the pediatric ward, I noticed a poster with photographs of "Second Year Pediatric Residents." I recalled the eleven residents I had so enjoyed meeting. But to my astonishment, the smiling faces didn't look at all like those residents. Confused, I hesitated, then asked my colleagues, "Is it true that just one year of residency changes people beyond recognition?" A roar of laughter greeted the question. Between laughs, the second-year resi-dents explained that there was a delay in updating the picture of the previous year's students. The tale of my confusion became the tradi-tional, welcoming icebreaker for pediatric residents new to GUH.

At GUH—which I joked meant Grueling, Unfair, and Human-less—I deepened my knowledge of children's illnesses, therapies, and cures, made dear friends, and sampled a mixture of life's sweetest and saddest experiences.

Determined to speak English with an "American" accent, I was in complete denial that the developmental cut-off age for acquiring flu-ency in a foreign language was long behind me. Brain elasticity in children and teens allows easy acquisition of languages. Scientists

ALLA SHAPIRO

FIG. 11. Georgetown University Hospital pediatric residents in 1994, my first year of residency in the US. I am second from the left in the second row. Despite the grueling hours on call and the lack of sleep, we showed support and affection for each other. *Photograph from the author's family collection.*

believe that puberty is a critical, transitional period in which automatic learning of language diminishes, and conscious learning is then required to master new language skills. *Your accent is here to stay*, I thought. Still, I had learned that "money talks," and, hoping that it did so without an accent, I hired an American language tutor.

Faking an American accent is no easy feat. Four weeks and four hundred dollars later, I started my rotation as a resident at Georgetown University Hospital's outpatient clinic. I was keen to test my linguistic skills. My first patient was Susan, a six-year-old with sparkling eyes and an independent attitude. Scheduled for a "well-child care visit," Susan politely shook my hand without skipping a beat in the song she hummed. I asked the girl and her mom a few routine questions, then examined her from head to toe to make sure that she was healthy and growing properly.

Susan, who waited until I paused, looked at her mom and declared, "Mommy, the doctor has an accent."

There goes four hundred dollars down the drain, was my first thought. Then my increased self-esteem canceled out that thought and I smiled. "Okay, you are right, Susan. You have three tries to guess what country my accent comes from."

"You are from France," Susan said bravely.

"No, I am not."

"You are from Poland." I sensed less confidence in Susan's voice.

"No, I am not."

Susan's mom watched the competition, apparently worried that without parental support her bright child might lose. "Listen to me, Sue. The doctor comes from the place from where your Uncle David's father came from."

"Yippee! The doctor is from New York!"

I instantly knew Susan had surpassed milestones for her age, and skipped the well-child exam questions to test psychological development.

I can still remember the exact moment when I was born again as an American physician. This transformation occurred during a night on call at the hospital for the first time as a pediatric resident. It proved as memorable as my worst first date. Ambulances raced in with little patients, their parents crying in fear. Stress levels soared on the night shift. The tension heightened as a personality clash

flared between me and Cristina, a senior resident with whom I was
paired on my first call.

Senior residents are supposed to guide and mentor less experienced colleagues, much like a pastor shepherds his flock, bringing
calm to crisis. They are encouraged to mitigate rookie panic attacks
by avoiding the application of such judgmental words as "psycho,"
"wacko," and "schizo" to subordinates. Senior residents are to help
less experienced associates become more mature and confident. Not
so, in my experience.

Cristina's reputation was consistent and notorious. She was
known as emotionally volatile, discourteous, and bossy. Her frequent
complaints, conveyed to the director of the Pediatric Residency Program, made situations look far worse than they were. After hearing
these complaints, the director would leave a note signed with her
own initials, DAR, inviting the resident-at-fault to her office for a
talk. Such visits were short, and never sweet.

On that first-call night I was shadowing Cristina, reading her
lips, and obeying all her commands. Late in the shift, a two-month-
old infant was admitted to the pediatric ward, running a fever and
crying endlessly. I felt a strong urge to soothe and cradle this baby
boy in my arms.

"Hold him still," Cristina commanded, "while I draw a few vials
of blood for the lab to test. The results might help us with the diagnosis and treatment." Cristina's authoritative tone made me tighten
my grip to restrain the baby so his movements would not be in the
way as she tried to access his tiny vein. She filled three vials, then
directed me to get ice to keep them cold until the lab technician
picked them up.

I knew that I could find ice from a refrigerator in a kitchen.

Therefore, I headed off to the kitchen, where nurses were having supper. I pulled an ice-cube tray from the freezer, unaware that I had just stepped back a few decades in time. I placed the tray on the countertop, noticing that the cubes appeared as old and misshapen as icebergs. I tried to free the ice cubes without spilling them, banging the tray.

The nurses began to stare at me. "What are you doing, Doctor?" asked one.

"I need ice!" I shouted. "I will be fired if I don't get this damn glacier to Cristina!"

Another nurse responded kindly. "Doctor, the ice-making machine is on this floor around the corner. It produces and dispenses ice cubes as well as crushed ice."

For a few seconds, I felt frozen in time. Cristina discovered that the baby's blood had spoiled from being too long at room temperature. Sure enough, the expected letter was in my locker the next day. My visit to the DAR's office stayed in my memory for years to come, along with the initials DAR.

I didn't have time for DC sightseeing during my busy residency and wasn't aware of the Daughters of the American Revolution (DAR) Constitution Hall. DAR is a women's service organization dedicated to promoting historic preservation, education, and patriotism, and to honoring the patriots of the Revolutionary War. The DAR building houses the largest concert hall in the District of Columbia. Designed for their annual convention, DAR Constitution Hall opened in 1929 and in 1985 was designated a National Historic Landmark building. Years after my residency, I received a letter in the mail with a bright logo and the letters "DAR." I nearly fainted.

"Again DAR? What did I do now?" I muttered as I nervously ripped the envelope. This time, the initials signaled better news: an invitation to my daughter Olga's high school graduation ceremony. I breathed a sigh of relief. *I have nothing to fear from DAR!*

Most doctors remember the years spent in residency as months of continuous sleep deprivation. They often tell funny stories—usually some years later—of things they did during those chronically sleep-starved years. My memory of my first time working at the pediatric unit as a resident for thirty-six hours was stamped by another typical occurrence for sleep-deprived physicians. After one particularly exhausting shift, when I was neither technically asleep nor fully awake, I tried to open someone else's car instead of my own in the hospital garage. After a long struggle maneuvering the keys, I became upset that I couldn't get into my car. I irritably concluded that the lock was faulty and called a locksmith. The amused locksmith pointed out that the keys I had in my hand would never open that car because I was trying to open someone else's Ford with my Nissan Altima keys.

Finally, I drove home, utterly spent, with several wasted hours added to my shift. This was when I realized that I had joined the ranks of medical residents across the USA who survived their first overnight shift. I was an American doctor in every sense.

CHAPTER 20

A Highway Legend (Escape from America's Most Wanted List)

My life in America offered me countless new things to learn, far greater freedoms—and endless things to misunderstand, such as driving rules. Most ordinary people in the Soviet Union did not own cars. Though we managed to acquire one a few years before we left, I never drove it.

I tackled learning to drive with the characteristic thoroughness that earned me success as a doctor, a mother, and all-around good person. The first route I mastered was my daily commute between Georgetown University at the edge of the Potomac River in Washington, and my suburban townhouse in Rockville, Maryland.

One late afternoon rush hour, I was driving my new car on a busy four-lane road. My concentration was laser focused on navigating my way home from work and following many recently-learned driving rules. I did fine with Rule Number 1: Stop at the red light. I stopped at one of the most congested intersections in the city. I waited for the green light, then dutifully followed Rule Number 2: "GO on green." I was unaware that safe driving sometimes means bending the official rules, using the good judgment that comes from experience.

In this case, Rule of Experience Number 2A was *DON'T* go on green when four cars ahead are filling up the intersection. Disregarding this unwritten rule would leave you stuck in the middle of the intersection, blocking four-way traffic until the traffic light changed again to green.

When the red light did change to green, I accelerated slowly, following the cars in front of mine. The first four cars pushed through on the green light, but I was left sitting in my car, stranded alone in the middle of the intersection, blocking traffic. I had firmly adhered to Rule Number 1 and stopped at the red light.

As I waited for the green light, I looked around curiously through my open windows and noticed that the atmosphere in the intersection was disorderly. Blocked by my car and trapped in the intersection, other drivers quickly morphed into wild animals desperate to escape their cages. Their loud, unfamiliar words, finger extensions, and vivid gestures gave me the impression that something was very wrong.

I handled this in the best way I knew—to "escape" by rolling up my windows and turning up the volume on the radio. When the light changed to green, I proceeded through the chaotic crossroad. For fifteen minutes my drive seemed uneventful. Then a loud noise interrupted my relative calm. I stuck by my trusted coping mechanism and turned the radio up louder. Then it occurred to me that it had been a while since I checked my rear and side mirrors, so I glanced clockwise at all three, as advised by the driver's manual. What I saw—or didn't see—startled me. No cars were behind me, or on either side. One of the area's busiest roads appeared completely deserted at the height of evening rush hour. A jarring noise much louder than those I had drowned out with my radio broke through the music, shaking me to the core: it was a police officer shouting into a megaphone for me to "STOP and pull over NOW."

Two police vehicles blocked my car within a tight triangle. Noise thundered from the levitating engines of two helicopters that seemed about to land on the roof of my car. Surrounded, I asked myself, *"What am I supposed to do next? Was there something in the manual that I missed?"* Expecting a command like "Put the gun on the ground and step away," I pulled over. The helicopters hovered above, synchronized with my car. A police officer emerged from his vehicle, gun drawn, and slowly approached me as I sat frozen in the driver's seat.

The next few minutes felt like hours. The officer stared at me, reported back to someone who likely was on high alert, then gestured me out of my car. His first question was, "Do you understand English?"

"Yes, Chief," I replied, praying that elevating the police officer's rank might keep me out of jail.

"Why didn't you pull over sooner? We have been chasing you for fifteen minutes," he demanded.

I did not want to admit that I always looked straight ahead, eyes on the road, when I drove, nearly oblivious to the rearview and side view mirrors. Quickly weighing a little white lie against honesty and the probable loss of my driver's license, I landed on a third option. "I was only trying to keep a safe distance between my car and your car behind me," I said, smiling weakly.

The policeman asked for my driver's license, my registration, and the model and year of my car. I expected his next question to be, "When were you discharged from a psychiatric facility?" Instead, after checking my credentials, the police officer simply told me that I was free to go if I promised to pull over immediately if I ever saw a police car following me again in the future. I waved good-bye, incredulous at my good fortune. "Thank you, Chief," I murmured.

For a few days, the whole episode seemed like a surreal dream. But when I was certain that I was, indeed, recalling true events, I shared it with a couple of my Georgetown pediatrician colleagues. Within hours, the story had spread far and wide by word of mouth, which was that era's version of viral, before cell phones, blogs, Facebook, or Twitter existed. As the account spread from one person to the next, it gathered descriptors: unforgettable, hilarious, and even legendary. The event was unrecognizable by the time it eventually returned to its main protagonist. By then, the story had some remarkable changes in narrative and outcomes. The most popular version featured a shooting spree with dead bodies on the scene. A manhunt along Wisconsin Avenue, police gunfire, overturned cars, and massive explosions characterized another version. My ego slightly bruised, I gratefully acknowledged that I had escaped a place on the "America's Most Wanted" list. I also added common sense to my own good driving rules.

CHAPTER 21

Taking Root in America

My life in the US combined making new friends and staying in touch with old ones. The friends that our Magnificent Seven made during their journey scattered once we reached the US. Our families exchanged phone calls and emails, and we shared stories about our cultural adjustments, the development of our children, and our career progress. Nothing came easily to any of us.

The first six years following our arrival in this country were nothing like a dancing party for Olga. She has only a few vague memories of arriving in the US at the age of six. She remembers the small townhouse we lived in and the constant fighting amongst the other six family members, which I attribute to the uncertainties of our lives then. Olga spent most of her time playing alone and trying to figure out the new language and culture.

The Jewish community that took us in and provided us with shelter also paid for our daughter to attend a private Jewish school for a few years. Unfortunately, the kids at the school were not as kind as the adults that placed her there. Olga was constantly teased for not knowing the language, wearing donated clothing, and not fitting in. For the first three years, she was isolated into an ESOL (English for

Students of Other Languages) classroom for much of the day. She
had an extremely difficult time in school and very few close friends.
Even so she, as all my family, are forever grateful to the Jewish community for adopting us and providing us with a home away from
home.

I constantly blamed myself for not giving Olga more time and
attention during this painful transition. But I asked myself, *How can
I listen to my daughter and comfort her if I do not have time to do it?* I
was spending one hundred hours per week at the hospital doing my
first year of residency-training in general pediatrics at the Georgetown University Hospital in Washington. (I calculated that my
annual salary at that time would have come to $1.05 per hour!) Still,
deep down, I did not feel that my onerous workload was reason
enough to excuse my behavior. I felt that postponing my care for
Olga simply meant neglecting my responsibility as her mother. Years
have passed, and I am still trying not to blame myself for the imbal-
ance between the demands of work and those of home, a perennial
predicament of all working mothers.

As Olga moved on to public school, she found a way to fit in. By
the end of college, she knew that she wanted to be a teacher. The
memory of her own hardships with schooling made it an easy decision to work with ESOL students.

American society helped define Olga in ways both quirky and
consequential. During her first few months at elementary school,
Olga decided from watching her American classmates that it was not
necessary to hang her jacket or coat in the closet. She just dropped
them on the floor in random locations. When Grandma Neli tried to
teach her to put her clothes away, Olga replied, "Grandma, you will
never be an American!" As seven-year-old Olga was getting dressed

to go with her parents to a party, I told her to wear "something casual." Olga replied, "*Potomac* casual? Or just casual?" In her mind, "Potomac casual" was the equivalent of Beverly Hills casual.

FIG. 12. Growing the next generation of space explorers. Olga is talking with one of the first American astronauts, Ronald Paris, in 1990. He instilled in her a desire to "fly high." *Photograph by Vadim Shapiro.*

Ever since Olga as a child met one of the first American astronauts at her dad's company picnic, she had wanted to fly high. She was fascinated by the stories the astronaut told about the space program. The company Olga's dad worked for had a long-standing relationship with the National Aeronautics and Space Administration (NASA), providing technical services ranging from weather observation to radar maintenance for all NASA's manned and unmanned spacecraft.

There was a sequel to this childhood encounter when she was attending college twelve years later.

Olga's habit was to call me from college every evening. During our regular conversations she provided three stock answers to my questions: "Yes. No. *Ffine.*" One night, Olga departed from the usual script when she added, "I love you." I returned the affection and didn't think about it until she called the next day, brimming with excitement. With no regard for the impact her shocking news would have, she told me that she had just landed in Delaware after her first skydive.

FIG. 13. Olga with her skydiving instructor in 2003. *Photograph by Delmarva Skydiving, Maryland.*

I was driving when I got this news. I ran a red light and then pulled over to recover. Olga enthused about the thrill of skydiving and promised to bring home a photograph and a video of her free fall. She said that, ever since she met the astronaut, skydiving had been on her list of not-to-be-missed life experiences. She added, "I decided to do it after you told me a couple of times, 'The choice is yours,' or, 'You decide about that.'"

This is my doing, I thought, with mixed feelings about the dangers that young adult independence brings. I had tried to be a wise parent who respected youthful cravings for self-determination. As a mother, I watched the drama of my daughter's growth with sympathy tempered with concern and respect. I empowered Olga to make her own choices whenever possible. In the long run, this approach worked well.

Olga now leads professional staff development at a high school in Montgomery County, Maryland. She collaborates with administrators and teachers to identify and support ways to improve student learning. Olga is up to the challenge. She is also involved in the "Focus" program, helping young people find and build career paths that best suit their aspirations, talents, and needs. The year-long experiential college-readiness educational curriculum is built on progressive development of key life skills to help students enhance individual development and incorporate what they learn into their everyday lives. For her efforts, Olga earned a Teacher of the Year Award.

Olga has dedicated herself to ensuring that the English language learners in her school never feel isolated or alone. In January of 2020 she presented a report to the board of education about the work she is doing to support English learners and how difficult school can be for these students without adult intervention. Although my daughter had a rough start in school, she believes that she can help students find their place as she did.

Olga now is a happily married mother of four adorable boys. Her husband, Pasha (Pavel Palanker), is a master sergeant retiring from active military service in the US Army. Pasha was awarded the Army Commendation Medal with V device for engaging and stopping a suicide bomber, as well as two Purple Hearts for injuries received in combat in Iraq.[35]

FIG. 14. My son-in-law, Pasha Palanker, is holding his purple hearts in his hands. *Photograph, 2019, by Alla Shapiro.*

"It's an individual award, but in my experience, it takes a 'village' to get a soldier through physical and emotional recovery," Pasha said in a speech accepting his second Purple Heart in late 2017. "If you are going through a tough time, be proactive, and if you need help, ask for it. Reach out to me, too. You will be amazed how much support you will get from people around you."

Pasha mirrors many of the qualities for which the bald eagle was chosen, in 1782, as the national emblem: freedom, great strength, and courage. The eagle has the ability to view things from a higher perspective. The spirit of this bird is said to appear during difficult times, not only to signal a new beginning, but to furnish the strength to endure difficulties.

Pasha also is from the former Soviet Union and has sacrificed a great deal for the country that he loves and now calls home.

FIG. 15. Family grows like branches on the tree. Olga and Pasha in 2019 with their children (clockwise from left to right): Sammy, Mikey, Nick, and Benji. *Photograph by Alla Shapiro.*

My mother's medical career in the US took a different route. In her late sixties, Neli switched from clinical work and research on kidney disease to the study of newly discovered molecules, work that led to innovative approaches likely to combat many diseases. For fourteen years, Neli worked in a team at the Molecular Recognition Section at the National Institutes of Health in Bethesda, Maryland. This group discovered compounds that would inhibit, or turn off, receptors on cell membranes that would otherwise be activated during injuries to some tissues and organs, exacerbating the damage.

At age ninety-four my mom remains active, curious, and fascinated with medical advances. She is a coauthor of numerous scientific

FIG. 16. Our grandma's name is Great. My mother, Neli Melman, in 2017 with her great-grandchildren (left to right): Nick, Sammy, and Mikey. *Photograph by Alla Shapiro.*

articles, and the author of several popular medical books, as well as a memoir, *Never Again*, which recounts her ordeal as a Holocaust survivor. The title is a vow to never allow repetition of such a genocide, in which an estimated six million Jews and five million non-Jewish people were killed by Adolf Hitler's Nazis.

More recently, Neli has been pursuing her hobby, painting. Her grandsons have "commissioned" works from her. She tells her great-grandchildren stories of their family's struggles and successes over the years. In this way, she shares with her boys the thrill of flying on the wings of time, creating links to the past and bridges to the future.

PART III

Looking Back
to Protect the Future

CHAPTER 22

Recipient of the "Order of the Nervous Neutron"

n the US I continued my career in pediatric hematology-oncology. In 1997, after completing my residency in general pediatrics at Georgetown University Hospital, I applied for a fellowship in pediatric hematology-oncology at the National Institutes of Health (NIH) in Bethesda, Maryland. Unlike other subspecialty training programs in the US, the first-year experience of fellows in this program was clinical, including both inpatient and outpatient care. During their second and third years, fellows could choose from a wide range of research opportunities at any scientific facility doing advanced research in oncology anywhere in the US.

Our class of fellows came from very different backgrounds. Now we shared the experience of working long, stressful hours. Frequent night shifts were often followed by full workdays. We naturally wanted to learn more about each other, and so the head of the Pediatric Hematology-Oncology Department suggested that each of us make a presentation on any topic we chose. The usual audience for such meetings was doctors and nurses and research staff.

I chose to speak about my experience as a medical first-responder at the worst nuclear disaster in history—the explosion in 1986 at the nuclear power station at Chernobyl, Ukraine. As the day of my presentation approached, I was nervous, replaying in my head many scenes from Chernobyl. I wondered, *How much should I tell the audience? Would they be even interested or care about this event?*

On the morning of the presentation, I entered a conference room at the NIH Clinical Center. The setting was familiar to me—big screen, projector, not many printed copies of my presentation. However, I was totally unprepared for the unfamiliar audience that faced me. I was expecting to see medical personnel wearing white coats or scrubs and walking shoes, suitable for spending long hours on their feet. To my surprise (and panic), most of the attendees were in military uniform.

Russian folklore has it that "Fear has big eyes." The saying applied to me that day. I still don't understand why military uniforms made me so nervous then. Perhaps it was because I hadn't seen them up close before and because I had no understanding of the army's hierarchy of rank. I assumed that they were all generals. (Even years later, my version of the story has the attendees as generals listening to my debut talk!) I tried to pluck up my courage.

The chief of the department read my mind and explained: "We usually put flyers about the upcoming NIH presentations at the campus information area. We also send newsletters to inform our neighbors across the street at the Armed Forces Radiobiology Research Institute (AFRRI), a place dedicated to radiation research and the leading institute in the country." He continued, "I guess they saw the topic of your talk and got interested in attending."

For the next hour, I presented my slides and recounted how I had treated traumatized children and families frightened to hysteria or shocked into silence. I orally painted for the quiet audience vivid images of these victims and the widespread destruction caused by the catastrophic nuclear accident. I exposed the true numbers: twenty-eight firemen and plant employees died in the immediate aftermath. Many suffered severe burns from uniforms soaked with radioactive water.

I described the fear that spread when we became aware of how many pieces of radioactive debris still remained on the reactor roof. The electronics in the robots initially used to clear wreckage were reduced to fried particles. After the robots failed, people were assigned to the task. Each Ukrainian volunteer received two thousand rubles—thirty-five dollars—to work on the roof for ninety seconds only. Risks and long-term consequences of radiation exposure were not mentioned. Dosimeters were confiscated to conceal the true scale of the disaster. For Soviet officials, the fear of panic was greater than the fear of radiation.

Very little national or international expertise on fighting graphite fires existed at that time. However, there was a great fear that any attempt to extinguish one might well result in further dispersion of radionuclides. A decision was made to layer the graphite fire with large amounts of different materials, each one designed to combat a different feature of the fire and the radioactive release. One of them was dolomite. Pilots dropped a total of six hundred tons from helicopters to smother the blazing reactor.

The pilots took an experimental drug by the name of indralin, a fast-acting compound, to shield them from the effects of the radiation. They also wore protective clothing, and their helicopters had been fitted with lead shielding, but neither protected them from their exposure to such deadly levels. One of the helicopter pilots developed leukemia after flying over the damaged reactor. He died in 1990 in the US at the Fred Hutchinson Cancer Research Center in Seattle, where he received a bone marrow transplant.

Because indralin was an experimental drug and likely of military importance to the Soviet government, I found limited information about it in Russian scientific journals. Several side effects of this drug stuck in my memory, including nausea, vomiting, and a drop in blood pressure—along with horrific images of what the pilots went through in their attempts to quench the burning reactor.

I finished my presentation. A few seconds of silence followed, then several hands rose into the air at once. The first question came from a physician who was also an air force colonel, Dr. Glen Reeves. Unlike typically-secretive Soviets, he was direct: "I am in charge of the radiation protection team at AFFRI. We are aware of all the experimental drugs against radiation exposure; however, I have never heard of indralin."

I sensed mild smugness in his voice. He was challenging me. I recalled that making eye contact is crucial for increasing perceived confidence. Looking him directly in the eyes, I spoke slowly and clearly: "This information is from a scientific journal. The article is in Russian. If you are interested, I will be happy to translate and email it to you."

His reply startled me. "No, thanks, I don't need the translation. Please email it to me in Russian and I will do it myself." I nodded in response. That same day I emailed the full article to the colonel. A week later he called me. There was no more condescension in his voice. Our conversation was brief. "Sorry to bother you. I tried to translate the article you sent me but failed. May I ask you to do it for me, please?" I agreed even before he finished the sentence.

I read each paragraph of the paper many times before putting it in writing. As a result, I ended up memorizing the whole article in two languages. In a few days I reported back to the colonel that I had completed the translation.

His next request came as a great surprise. "Could you please bring the translated article to my office at AFRRI? I will meet you here and show you the facility."

I said, "Of course! Thank you for this extraordinary opportunity!" In my enthusiasm, I had responded in Russian, but my newfound friend the colonel got the message.

Our meeting was unforgettable. I noticed a few computer screens in his office. One of the screen savers displayed a message: "Jesus is resurrected." I was surprised not by the message, but by the fact that the words flew by in Russian!

Now it was my turn to ask questions. "Where did you learn Russian?" I asked.

The colonel stretched in his chair as he prepared to tell me a long story. "I spent a few years in the Urals, USSR, studying reports on several hundred workers at the Mayak plutonium production facility. It was being used for weapons." While the English translation of *mayak* is, ironically, lighthouse, it and the other plants were surrounded by "secret cities." He said that the locations and addresses of those places were merely numbers appended to the city name. The radioactive liquid wastes were emptied directly into the Techa River.

"When the first reports on the chronic radiation skin injuries in workers became available, much of the scientific world was skeptical. No such syndrome had been described in the West. The most frequent complaints in villagers were headache, dizziness, increased tiredness, disturbances of mood, and decreased appetite."

I listened to his testimony in disbelief. I had spent thirty-five years of my life in the USSR and had never heard of plants processing fuel for weapons near any big cities in Russia. Yet in just one year in the Soviet Union my new friend from AFRRI had learned all about the underground tanks with highly concentrated wastes that had exploded in 1957 and contaminated a large area.

The colonel said, "I spoke personally with Soviet scientists who admitted, off the record, that they sometimes left their dosimeters at home when they knew they would be exposed to higher than normal levels of radiation. Some of these individuals had one set of records (the accurate ones) for their personal knowledge and one set for safety personnel." The colonel paused to allow me to digest this. I tried to replace it with a positive comment, but I couldn't find any.

He picked up where he left off. "I also heard anecdotes of persons being given 'administrative' doses, that is, when their actual exposure exceeded daily or annual limits, a number at or just below the standard was recorded instead." My new amazing friend must have been fluent in Russian to understand the anecdotes and unspoken meanings that are only read or heard between the lines. The colonel then summarized his dark stories:

"In June 1992, three years after the veil of Soviet secrecy was lifted, I participated in a historic workshop that was conducted at George Mason University in Fairfax, Virginia. This event, underwritten by AFRRI and the Department of Energy, brought together scientists and political figures from both the Russian Federation and the United States. Because of those and subsequent discussions, we collaborated on studying the effects of chronic radiation exposure on the Techa River village populations, which became the springboard for further research."

The colonel then rose from his chair, signifying that our conversation, peppered with a mix of English and Russian, was over. He said, "Now I'll explain the general scope of the AFRRI mission to you, and then we will go down to the basement to see the nuclear reactor."

The images of the Chernobyl disaster were still alive in my

memory, yet I found the colonel's voice calming as he told me about AFRRI. Fascinated, I concentrated with my full attention as I learned about the purpose of AFRRI, their tasks, assignments, and collaborations. All their effort is directed toward a single goal: to preserve and protect the health and performance of US military personnel through research and training that advances understanding of the effects of ionizing radiation. They also maintain a pool of qualified radiation biologists to develop measures to prevent, assess, and treat radiation injury. The colonel paused.

I felt an intense, almost physical, sensation of sadness for the losses that had occurred during and in the aftermath of Chernobyl. The burn of emotional pain was almost as strong as a radiation burn. *What if Soviet officials had not hidden the truth from their people? What if the doctors had known the signs and consequences of radiation exposure? What if? What if?* These questions were difficult and the answers didn't matter anymore.

The colonel must have sensed my feelings. "Let's see the nuclear reactor in action," he suggested.

Although I was not in the best mood for the proposed "show," I followed him to the closed area deep down the stairs, and we entered a large underground room. My AFRRI friend Colonel Reeves gave a mini-lecture about the TRIGA (Training, Research, Isotopes, General Atomic) nuclear reactor, which was the basis for the existence of AFRRI (established by Secretary Robert McNamara in 1961). I listened with fascination about the features of TRIGA. The colonel explained that the reactor could pulse radiation and thus simulate the radiation characteristics of various nuclear weapons.

When we entered the underground room, the core of the reactor was in a deep-water pool. The colonel whispered something into the ear of a technician. In the next moment, the reactor control rods quickly rose from the bottom of the pool, and a burst of blue light occurred. The control rods were immediately dropped back into place to cool off the reaction. I breathed a sigh of relief. The colonel sensed my anxiety and smiled—a sign of reassurance that everything was going according to design. I looked at the person who was operating the reactor. His facial expression suggested that he really enjoyed alarming visitors!

"You deserve our certificate for bravery," announced the colonel.

That is how I became the recipient of the "Order of the Nervous Neutron" certificate.

FIG. 17. In 1998, after I anxiously watched a simulated nuclear reaction at the US Armed Forces Radiobiology Research Institute, Colonel Glen Reeves handed me a custom-made certificate entitled "Order of the Nervous Neutron," showing a rattlesnake superimposed over an atom that is spitting out particles and photons! *Photograph by Alla Shapiro.*

CHAPTER 23

Children of Chernobyl

U pon my arrival in the US in 1989, luxuries like perfumes and beauty salons were far from my mind. Therefore, I missed the creation and launch that same year of Red Door Perfume—a classic and elegant signature fragrance, symbolizing glamor and luxury for women around the world. A few years later, someone introduced this already-iconic perfume to me, along with the name of its creator, Elizabeth Arden.

Florence Nightingale Graham, who went by the business name of Elizabeth Arden, was a Canadian born businesswoman who founded and built a cosmetics empire in the United States. Born on December 31, 1878, she died at the age of eighty-seven in Manhattan, New York, on October 18, 1966. A pioneer in the advertising of beauty aids, Elizabeth Arden opened many stylish salons in the US and around the world. At the time of her death there were one hundred Arden beauty salons throughout the world.

In 1998, during my second year of fellowship in pediatric hematology-oncology at the National Institutes of Health (NIH), Bethesda, I received an unexpected offer from a colleague, one of the attending physicians from the pediatric ward. He greeted me in the hallway and started the following conversation:

"My family lives in Ireland, and I just spoke with one of my relatives in Dublin. He told me that Paul Newman, the famous actor, has started a center there where children from Ukraine and Belarus can stay for expert medical attention and recuperation. The center is based at a five-hundred-year-old Irish castle that belonged to Elizabeth Arden. When she died, the Irish government bought the castle, but later turned it over to Paul Newman, who converted the castle and its grounds into the Barretstown Castle Centre."

I listened attentively to these astonishing facts, wondering why my colleague was telling me all this. I soon found out.

"Most of the children have suffered from leukemia or lymphoma," the doctor continued. "They live in Ukraine and Belarus and were diagnosed and treated after the Chernobyl disaster. After achieving first remission, they will come to Ireland for recuperation and any expert medical attention they need."

I asked, "Can I do anything to help these children?"

"Of course, you can! We will assign you to participate in this program. It's sponsored by Chernobyl Children's Project International. The charity was founded in 1991 by Adi Roche, who is a humanitarian, activist, and campaigner for nuclear disarmament."[36]

My next question was, "Where am I going?"

"You are going to spend a few weeks at a camp in Ireland working with these children. The venue is Barretstown Castle Centre. The doctors and children need you there, Alla. You speak Russian and Ukrainian; therefore, you will help English-speaking staff members communicate with the kids. Your pediatric-hematology skills will also be of great value. Though all the children are supposed to be in remission from lymphoma or leukemia, you will apply your professional skills in case any of their symptoms recur. In addition, some of the children will require regular blood tests to help monitor their remission, and you will help to interpret the results."

I surprised the doctor by saying, "I know about that place! The castle belonged to Elizabeth Arden, and all the doors are still painted red."

When I arrived at the camp, I was astonished by the beauty of setting and the castle, where all the medical personnel lived (the children stayed in adjacent houses). During the five years after Elizabeth Arden acquired it in 1962, she reconstructed, redecorated, and refurnished it. Her influence remains obvious to this day.

FIG. 18. Elizabeth Arden, of Red Door Perfume fame, acquired this Irish castle in 1962. When she died, the Irish government bought the castle, then sold it to Paul Newman for one dollar in 1986. Newman converted the castle and its grounds into the Barretstown Castle Center, where child victims of the Chernobyl accident could recuperate after treatment for leukemia and lymphoma. I worked at this camp for two weeks in 1998 as a doctor and translator. *Photograph by Alla Shapiro.*

I spent more than two weeks at Paul Newman's extraordinary camp. I and three other physicians from Spain and the UK cared for over forty children. The entire staff infused the children's lives there with love, acceptance, and compassion, and they treated their young charges to thrilling adventures, such as horseback riding and hot air balloon escapes.

Paul Newman continued to support projects for the children of Chernobyl until his death in 2008.

CHAPTER 24

The Pursuit of One Gram of Indralin

After I was awarded the certificate of the "Order of the Nervous Neutron," I became a frequent visitor at the Armed Forces Radiobiology Research Institute (AFRRI). The scientists and laboratory staff were designing experiments to test new drug candidates in different stages of development. They would give two groups of mice the same lethal doses of radiation. One group would receive the experimental drug and the other would not. If the drug did not seem to give the first group a survival advantage, the drug would never make it past that stage. What the scientists lacked were ways to reproduce the effects of such a drug in a real-world setting.

At the time of the Chernobyl accident, a drug called indralin was in the experimental phase in the Soviet Union. It had shown positive results in lab animals given high doses of radiation. However, when it was given to the helicopter pilots to protect them from radiation, it was not effective. Nevertheless, the scientists at AFRRI still thought the drug had potential benefits. After my presentation in which I mentioned indralin, they asked me, "Could you help us get one gram of indralin from the Soviets?"

By 1998, even though I had grown used to hearing straightforward questions, I replied hesitantly, "I think I can." Then I said, "I will do my best to obtain indralin for your laboratory."

I decided to contact my former department chief in Kiev on his home number. Without politely inquiring about his work, health, and family, I got right to the point and asked, "Could you please provide an acclaimed institution in the US with one gram of indralin? I did not want to hear no, so I promptly continued, "This is the best facility in the US for conducting experiments to test drugs that might protect humans from radiation. They have the best equipment and personnel for this research."

He replied, "I will call one academician in Moscow tomorrow. He would know who has indralin. I will tell him that you need it, and he will mail a package to you." I felt overwhelmingly surprised and tried to clarify my request.

"Thank you. I am happy to hear this," I said, keeping my voice businesslike and trying to suppress my excitement. "What are the terms?"

He said, "I will let you know tomorrow after my conversation with Moscow."

The next day the professor called me and said, "You will receive one gram of indralin for free. Moscow is presenting this as a gift to the US scientists. The only condition is that the US scientists must share the results of their experiments with Russian scientists. Fair enough?"

"Yes, yes!" I said. The terms are acceptable! AFRRI will send a letter to Moscow confirming it. I will talk to them tomorrow."

The AFRRI team leader whose group was responsible for the experiments promised to draft a letter to the academician in Moscow the next day, then show it to me before mailing. A few days later, I received a draft of the letter from AFRRI. Everything looked great: the letter included such words as "grace" and "honor" and "indebtedness." Only one piece was missing: the promise that AFRRI scientists would share the results of the experiments involving indralin. I commented on this and accepted the team leader's apologies, as well as his assurance that the omission was a mistake. He said, "I will add the missing part now and our director will sign it before the letter goes out."

I waited a long time to hear back from AFRRI. Then I called the team leader to insist that they amend the letter and mail it as soon as possible. I thought, *There might not be another chance like this. Don't they get it?* Weeks went by. According to the AFRRI team, the letter was in the director's office awaiting his signature.

One chilly day in February 1998, when I prepared myself to call AFRRI with another reminder to mail the letter off to Moscow, the Kosovo crisis in Yugoslavia shook the world. In that year, following the breakup of Yugoslavia, growing ethnic violence in Kosovo, promoted by the Kosovo Liberation Army (KLA), led Serbian leader Slobodan Milosevic to launch a counterinsurgency campaign against the ethnic Albanian and Kosovar communities in Kosovo. By February of that year, Kosovo was embroiled in a full-scale civil war.

Russia, with its longstanding interests in Yugoslovia, opposed the intervention of the United States in this conflict, and the relationship between the two superpowers deteriorated. American diplomats in Moscow moved out of Russia. Along with the diplomatic channels, scientific and cultural connections between two countries were damaged. Russia pulled their scientists, sportsmen, and even ballet performers out of the US. All my efforts to establish productive and collegial interactions between the two countries came to nothing. The opportunity to obtain indralin through my contact was lost, but not forgotten.

CHAPTER 25

Triumph

A New Drug

I was slowly getting over my shattered dream of testing indralin and using it to treat patients exposed to radiation. Nevertheless, I resolved not to give up entirely. I was a second-year fellow in the pediatric oncology program at the National Institutes of Health (NIH), doing research at Bethesda Naval Hospital (currently Walter Reed) in Bethesda, Maryland, and I was assigned to study the drug in patients with prostate cancer.

Each group in this study received an investigational drug, genistein, a compound found in soybeans. The rationale for holding a clinical trial on it appeared strong: overall data based on Asian women, mainly derived from case-control studies, showed a dose-dependent, statistically significant association between soy food intake and breast cancer risk reduction.[37] In addition, animal experiments conducted in the US suggested that genistein held promise for preventing cancer in humans.[38] The anticancer properties of genistein had been demonstrated in animal models of breast cancer.[39] Moreover, in a relatively large number of potentially metastatic cases, the progression of cancer was suppressed by genistein.

The results of the study conducted at the naval hospital confirmed that the doses of genistein that patients received were not harmful and did not cause any side effects. We obtained and analyzed a variety of data from these studies to better navigate further clinical trials in patients with other cancers, especially advanced prostate cancer.

I was excited to learn more about genistein, its diverse biological activities, and how this soybean extract could be used in medicine. One of the mechanisms of action drew my attention: multiple scientific articles suggested that genistein is a potent antioxidant, a critical feature for any drug intended to reduce the damaging effects on tissues of radiation. *Bingo!* I whispered to myself. *We should try using genistein to protect mice from death caused by lethal doses of radiation.*

I talked to Dr. Chris Takimoto, a senior investigator at the National Cancer Institute (and an assistant professor of medicine at the Uniformed Services University of the Health Sciences), who was my supervisor. "Would you please allow me to take one gram of genistein from our laboratory and give it to AFRRI? They could test it in mice first to ascertain if it protects lab animals from death by lethal doses of radiation."

"Let's do it," my boss replied with confidence.

The next day three scientists from AFRRI visited our laboratory at the hospital. The meeting was a brainstorming session, exciting and productive. Our colleagues from the institute across the street left our facility carrying one precious gram of genistein. This collaboration launched a new series of experiments at AFRRI. As one of the fans and supporters of this initiative, I followed their progress daily.

The team gave lethal doses of radiation to two groups of mice. One group was protected with genistein, and the other group was not. The scientist in charge of this project was responsible for assessing the animals' behavior and monitoring signs that would signal deterioration leading to their demise.

During the first days of the experiment, I was impatient, and I often annoyed my AFRRI colleagues with questions such as, "How many are still alive?" until one of the researchers explained, "We are not expecting to see deaths of any animals until day fifteen to twenty, after their exposure to radiation. If genistein works, the majority of mice in this group will be alive by day thirty after they were irradiated."

"What will happen to the animals who did not take genistein?" I asked.

I was disappointed but not surprised by his answer. "Our past experiments showed that all animals exposed to high doses of radiation without receiving any drugs to protect them died."

I marked day number fifteen on my calendar and started to cross out the days as they passed. Exactly on the critical day, light snow and a wintry mix started falling over parts of Washington and Maryland. By the next morning, heavy snow and ice covered the area, and the National Weather Service had issued ice storm and winter storm warnings for some areas. The full misery of winter weather swept through Washington, closing schools and shuttering government offices as snow gave way to sleet and freezing rain. As I was contemplating these weather scenarios, my phone rang.

"Hey, Alla, listen," came the familiar voice of my AFRRI colleague, a PhD who led the project team. "Our offices and laboratories are closed, so nobody from personnel will appear at work. As a result, the mice will not get any food or water until weather permits and roads are clear."

I anticipated his message: "And they all will die not from radiation, but from hunger."

My colleague did not respond, and I interpreted his silence as consent. My own statement made me start crying.

My tearful voice triggered the following response from my colleague: "Calm down, please. I have a four-wheel drive car and will go to the lab to feed all the poor animals. In case genistein fails to protect them, we will have strong evidence that the mice died of radiation, and not from starvation."

For the next few hours, I tried to stay calm, staring out the window waiting for the snow to stop. In the meantime, my colleague successfully accomplished his mission, which had seemed almost hopeless a few hours ago.

The final results of this experiment were remarkable: in the genistein-treated group, sixty-nine percent of the mice survived. The dose of radiation that they received would otherwise have been lethal. There were no adverse effects, compared with the group that did not receive treatment. Everyone on the team celebrated the success. We declared "survivor-mice" as a special group. Never before had experimental mice received food and water from the hands of a PhD who made it through a snowstorm to take care of them and strengthen the protection they received from genistein.

A few months later, the experiment was modified. A new group of mice received only one under-the-skin injection of genistein twenty-four hours after radiation exposure. The results exceeded all expectations: eighty-eight percent of the treated mice survived.

Our team of coinventors, consisting of scientists and doctors from AFRRI and NIH, filed a patent application for this invention. The abstract states, "The present invention provides compositions and methods for the prophylactic and therapeutic treatment of animals, including humans, from radiation injury. In particular, the present invention provides methods and compositions comprising the isoflavone genistein."[40]

Between 2010 and 2013 additional patents involving the prophylactic and therapeutic use of genistein were granted in the US, Canada, European countries, and Australia.[41]

Recently, a new and more effective formulation of genistein was created, and it has a new name: BIO 300. Experiments in mice and monkeys, and clinical trials in humans, have been conducted with this formulation.[42] BIO 300 is regarded as a medical countermeasure for use in the event of a radiological or nuclear incident. It is also being developed to mitigate the delayed effects of acute radiation exposure to the lungs.[43] The lungs are especially prone to damage from radiation exposure, which can lead to debilitating and life-threatening diseases including pneumonitis and pulmonary fibrosis. Currently, there are no drugs approved to prevent or treat radiation-induced lung injury. BIO 300 is in a phase I/II clinical trial in lung cancer patients being treated with radiation and chemotherapy. This trial is assessing the drug's ability to protect patients' lungs from toxicities caused by radiation used to treat tumors.[44]

I continued my collaboration with AFRRI for many years. I taught courses to my military colleagues, presented my work at scientific conferences, and served on scientific panels discussing the protective effects of new treatments against radiation damage. In appreciation for my work, I was awarded a beautiful plaque containing an eternal Lichtenberg tree. The tree is created by high-energy

FIG. 19. High voltage Lichtenberg tree. The tree is made by bombarding insulating plastic with high-energy electrons, creating minuscule fractures in the form of a tree. No two trees are alike. The US Armed Forces Radiobiology Research Institute gave me this plaque in appreciation for my work. Over many years I taught courses to my military colleagues, presented papers at scientific conferences, and served on scientific panels discussing new treatments against radiation damage. *Photograph, 1998, by Alla Shapiro.*

electron bombardment onto insulating plastic, creating minuscule fractures in the form of a tree. No two trees are alike.

This one-of-a-kind acknowledgement of my scientific contributions will always be a source of inspiration for my future work. I never fail to marvel at the burst of atomic energy frozen in time in this beautiful image.

However, nothing amazed me more than the people whom I met at AFFRI. Colonel (Dr.) Andrew Huff, an AFRRI director for six years, stood out as a professional and an individual. Andrew's professional skills in forensic psychiatry and aerospace medicine are complemented by his equally remarkable humanity. I think that there is nothing more dignifying in a physician than the ability not only to heal but to encourage others.

CHAPTER 26

Chernobyl

Twenty Years After

I n 2006, seventeen years after arriving in Washington, I flew back to Kiev, the country I thought I had left for good. I mused over the many changes that had taken place since then, in my own life and in the world. Kiev was revitalized, boasting restaurants and hotels that had been renovated to become trendy hang-outs for wealthy Europeanized locals.

During the flight, an American gentleman seated next to me interrupted my thoughts: "I'm on my way to visit Pripyat, the ghost town near Chernobyl. It's a hot destination now. How about you?" I answered, "That's not for me," to which my neighbor reacted with raised eyebrows.

I was not in a mood to explain my far-from-enthusiastic response. I was on my way to give a speech at an international conference marking the twentieth anniversary of the Chernobyl nuclear disaster, at which I would represent the Office of Counter-Terrorism of the US Food and Drug Administration.

It was a great honor to receive the letter of invitation from the Ukraine Ministry of Health. Above the respectful "Dear Doctor," I noticed a *tryzub* (Ukrainian trident), the ubiquitous symbol of modern Ukraine. How starkly that elegant invitation contrasted with the wrinkled piece of paper that declared me "a citizen of no nation." *I've come a long way,* I thought.

The meeting revived a painful memory of something that happened shortly after the Chernobyl disaster. I was introduced to the head of the Ukrainian Ministry of Health. Before me stood the very minister who had summarily dismissed me, because of my Jewish name and heritage, as a candidate for a top position at a new institute to study the effects of radiation. This time, he greeted me as an honored guest.

The conference took place at the National Opera House of Ukraine, regarded as one of the most magnificent buildings in the country. At the meeting, I presented novel approaches to the development of medications for large populations exposed to high doses of radiation from radiation accidents, as well as nuclear terrorist attacks.

Traditionally, to test the effectiveness of an experimental drug, one group of patients with a particular disease or condition receives the drug and another group does not. Their results are then compared. However, subjecting humans to high doses of radiation in order to study the efficacy of a drug intended to mitigate the effects of that radiation is neither ethical nor feasible. That is why in 2002 the FDA implemented the Animal Rule, under which the effectiveness of new drugs against high doses of radiation, as well as biological or chemical threat agents, can be tested on animals. Properly designed and well-controlled animal studies allow the benefits of the drug to be assessed, then extrapolated to humans.

The FDA worked with other government agencies to advance the development and availability of medical countermeasures (MCMs).[45]

One such partnership was between the Office of Counter-Terrorism at the FDA and the National Institute of Allergy and Infectious Diseases (NIAID), at the National Institutes of Health (NIH), which helps to plan and conduct preclinical and clinical studies. In my talk I mentioned NIAID's contributions to the research.

Dr. Bert Maidment, an associate director at NIAID, was in charge of the Radiation and Nuclear Countermeasures Program. Bert's team members were responsible for planning our joint meetings and for follow-up communication. Mutual respect created camaraderie between our teams and long-lasting friendships.

I will always remember the twenty minutes of sheer joy and pride I experienced during my talk. I had a strong belief that, instead of listening to me, people in the audience were reading my name badge. Its simplicity of design spoke volumes and meant the world to me.

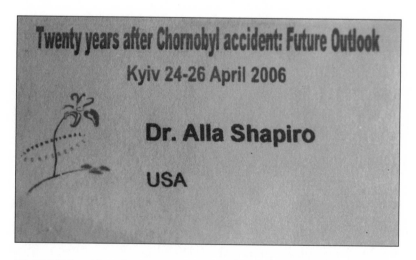

FIG. 20. With pride in being an American, I wore this badge throughout a 2006 international conference, held in Kiev, marking the twentieth anniversary of the Chernobyl nuclear disaster. *Photograph by Alla Shapiro.*

During my trip, I found it impossible to share in the spirit of the new Kiev. Along with my friends and former colleagues, I couldn't shake off images of the devastation in Pripyat, the former secret Soviet city closed to anyone but workers at the Chernobyl nuclear reactor and their families. Forty-nine thousand people were forced to evacuate the day after Chernobyl's Reactor No. 4 exploded on April 26, 1986. Visitors can still see the detritus of lives interrupted. Empty classrooms are scattered with open books; toys, laundry, and decorations remain exactly where they were left.

Today Chernobyl appeals to tourists who wish to explore a place that has been completely abandoned by humans for nearly thirty years; they want to find out what an apocalyptic world might look like. "Excellent private tours in the Chernobyl exclusion zone" are now widely offered. They guarantee that visitors will have "a great experience witnessing horrific changes this event imposed upon the local landscape as well as the inhabitants." The guides calm fears about exposure to radiation by assuring tourists that any high levels on their body would be detected by the machines they must pass through on the way out of Chernobyl's exclusion zone. Those machines—old Soviet steel contraptions that look like retro airport metal detectors—hardly inspire confidence.

I thought, *I don't need to see it again. I saw it all when it happened.* On my return flight home, I had flashbacks to the aftermath of the explosion that had such a profound impact on my life and the lives of so many others. That catastrophic event shaped the person I am today. Emotions of shame, anger, and helplessness have been replaced with knowledge and confidence. Now we are better prepared to respond to nuclear disasters, and we have more interventions to prevent and treat radiation injuries.

Until my retirement in August 2019, I continued to work as a medical officer at FDA, evaluating drug candidates to treat people who have been exposed to harmful levels of radiation.[46]

CHAPTER 27

On the Shoulders of Giants

I continued to develop professionally in the United States, free from the anti-Semitism and other cruel aspects of my former life in the Soviet Union. I was fulfilling my commitment after Chernobyl to focus on the treatment of victims of accidental radiation exposure.

I am well aware that many careers, like mine, were built on the shoulders of giants. My accomplished predecessors' legacies moved me up each rung in the competitive fields of medicine and biomedical research so that I was able to reach top positions in key organizations.

Marie Sklodowska-Curie was among the titans I admired most. Curie is known as the mother of modern chemistry and physics, and today remains the most widely recognized female scientist. Born in Poland in 1867, Madam Curie was the first woman to win a Nobel Prize, and the only woman to win Nobels in two different fields: physics and chemistry. Marie's efforts, together with those of her husband, Pierre Curie, led to the discovery of the radioactive elements polonium and radium. The couple fearlessly dove headfirst into their research, with no protection from the invisible rays, which she fondly called "fairy light." In 1919 one gram of radium, valued at one hundred thousand dollars, was presented to Madam Curie as a gift from the people of the United States. A decade later, President Herbert Hoover awarded her prize money, which she used to acquire another gram of precious radium.

My fascination with Marie Curie's brilliant life goes back to my middle school years in Kiev, Ukraine. In the seventh grade we began learning Dmitry Mendeleev's chart for organizing chemical elements. Our chemistry teacher, who admired Madam Curie, spent the entire lesson talking exclusively about Marie's life and her discoveries, which changed the world of science. As a result, upon graduation from high school, I had a significant gap in my knowledge of the periodic table. I thought that it consisted only of two elements, radium and polonium—the latter named by Marie Curie in honor of Poland. My former chemistry teacher was eventually fired for not doing her job; however, I learned a lot from her about Marie's genius, triumphs, and tragedies.

Despite the many honors that were heaped on her, Marie remained humble and science-focused, using substantial prize money to further her research. In the course of that work, Marie routinely carried objects that glowed with radiation in the pockets of her standard lab coats. More than eighty years after her death, her laboratory gloves and paper notes, which are sealed in a lead-lined box, still emit radiation.

Curie endured tragic loss (her husband, Pierre, died in a street accident eleven years after they married), ridicule, and the prejudice against women in science that was prevalent in her time. She met Albert Einstein during her career, and he remained one of her most supportive friends and confidants for the rest of her life. In times of turmoil, Marie often turned to him for counsel, comfort, and support.

That timeless genius was a model of kindness, compassion, and strength. Einstein's unparalleled intellect was accompanied by a great generosity of spirit. The discoveries that Curie made so many years ago gave us a greater understanding of atoms. Her pioneering research led to the current use of high energy radioactive materials to treat cancer patients.

In 2011 I attended the 14th International Congress in Radiation Research in Warsaw and Krakow, titled "Science as a Public Duty: Following the Ideas and Work of Maria Sklodowska-Curie." The event was organized by the Institute of Nuclear Physics of the Polish Academy of Sciences and the Polish Radiation Research Society. It brought together politicians, scientists, and about three hundred Marie Curie researchers at the Palace of Culture and Science. The conference included a contest for the most innovative ways of promoting science. The atmosphere was alive with excitement and fun as participants celebrated the one-hundredth anniversary of Madam Curie's Nobel Prize in Chemistry.

At one of the conference workshops, I gave a presentation on behalf of the Counter-Terrorism and Emergency Coordination Staff of the Center for Drug Evaluation and Research of the US Food and Drug Administration. I emphasized the FDA's role in the nation's capability of "fostering development of medical products to respond to deliberate and naturally emerging public health threats."[47] In my talk, I highlighted progress in the development of drugs against radiation exposure, and stressed the importance of testing these experimental drugs in cancer patients who were undergoing radiation treatment. I said that doctors and scientists hoped that properly used drugs could protect patients from radiation exposure and simultaneously kill malignant tumors. This promising dual approach has received significant support from the international community of experts.

After I addressed the US government's concerns about terrorist threats to the US, there was an intense exchange regarding possible radiation exposure scenarios. One of the attendees asked, "Could you name the most destructive nuclear devices, please?"

I said, "The concern is about the possible detonation of a nuclear weapon by a terrorist group in a major city, in particular the explosion of a ten-kiloton nuclear bomb. It would cause significant loss of lives and lots of serious injuries; explosions would produce fires throughout the immediate blast zone." The audience was silent, captivated by what they heard. I proceeded to the conclusion: "An explosion in a large city would result in an estimated 450,000 to 700,000 displaced persons flooding into nearby states. The economic impact on the country would be hundreds of billions of dollars, and the estimated time of recovery would be decades."

"You obviously have more questions," I said. Lots of hands were raised into the air. I tried to respond to the broad range of questions.

"The US government is prepared to respond to a nuclear attack. National and state level exercises are regularly conducted. Military, medical, and civilian personnel are trained to prevent and treat radiation injuries. In the case of a nuclear detonation, they will help potential victims evacuate or shelter in place in the immediate fallout path. The media are poised to provide effective communication of instructions to the affected population."

I backed up these statements by talking about my participation in national- and state-level preparedness exercises that are regularly conducted by government agencies in the US. Cutting-edge science and technology support efforts to advance progress in this area.

The closing question was critical. "Do we have medications and necessary supplies for radiation emergency situations?"

I proudly explained, "In the US there is a national repository of life-support medications and medical/surgical items to treat patients in case of medical emergencies, including terrorist-perpetrated chemical, biological, radiological/nuclear, or explosive incidents. These critical medications and supplies, stored in the Strategic National Stockpile (SNS), are ready for use. These SNS assets can be delivered as "push packages" to any of the states or US territories within twelve hours of a federal decision to deploy.[48]

As I finished my presentation, I held my breath and took a moment to feel momentarily flooded with gratitude for the country I live in. Little did I realize that I would have to revisit my endorsement of the Strategic National Stockpile's preparedness for national disaster.

Ten years later, in early spring of 2020, the coronavirus (COVID-19) pandemic struck. Life for some came to a standstill, while front-line workers faced a frightening new reality. In summer 2020, first responders were still scrambling to get personal protective gear, and patients often lacked life-saving equipment and medications. The SNS was depleted.

CHAPTER 28

Who Will Live and Who Will Die?

I returned home from my trip to Poland inspired by Marie Curie's accomplished but tragic life. Throughout her years of dedicated research, she remained unaware of radiation's dark side. She used radium "gloss" at a reception in France to demonstrate the luminous element's ability to distinguish real from imitation diamonds. Radium caused the real stones, but not the false ones, to burst into brilliant light in a dark room. It is likely that she had additional radiation exposure during World War I when she oversaw the French X-ray ambulance service and also trained technicians. Marie Curie died at age sixty-seven of aplastic anemia, which probably was caused by long-term radiation exposure.

For several weeks, starting with my Poland trip, I was feeling very tired. After I fainted at the gym, I decided that it was time to see a doctor. In January of 2011, I was recovering from anesthesia after a diagnostic procedure when the physician who performed it concluded that I had colon cancer.

After the procedure, the doctor entered my room. He looked straight into my eyes and, without sparing my feelings or hesitating, conveyed an excruciating diagnosis. Like anyone in that situation, I reacted with shock and disbelief, followed by anxiety, anger, and depression.

I was still feeling groggy when he called my primary care doctor, who happens to be my best friend and one of the best doctors in the area. Dr. Irene Feldman promptly contacted two of her colleagues, a surgeon and an oncologist. After presenting them with my case, she arranged appointments with both specialists for me. Timely surgery, performed by a brilliant surgeon, was my first step toward recovery.

The skilled doctor presented treatment options and formed a treatment plan for me. I became a member of his team, and slipped into an adjustment phase, during which I reflected a great deal on doctor-patient relations. I anticipated a bright future for myself because I believed that I would receive the right treatment in an expedient manner.

My memories of treating patients in Kiev came back to me with new clarity. I especially remembered three innocent children: three pairs of eyes full of hope, and three sets of parents begging for help. The two girls, six and ten years old, and a boy who was three at that time, had acute leukemia, the most common cancer in children and teens across the world. Each of them required ten days of intense chemotherapy, for which we needed thirty vials of the same drug.

I approached the head nurse of our pediatric hematology department and asked her to supply thirty vials of cytarabine by the next day. She replied, "We don't have thirty vials on our ward or in the entire hospital. I have seventeen. You figure out who will receive the treatment and for how many days."

To undertake that task would have violated my principles. Therefore, I called for help. My boss, the professor, scratched his head. "Please, think harder," I implored.

The professor hesitated as I followed his eye movements, trying to read his mind. I anticipated his intention to divide equally the seventeen vials of the drug so that each child would receive an uninterrupted ten-day treatment course. After a few minutes of unsuccessful mental arithmetic, the professor gave up and said, "I need to talk to the top hospital authorities about how best to distribute the drug."

"How could hospital administrators help you to choose?" I asked.

He did not answer, but assured me that he would see me the next day at work.

The next morning Svetlana, one of the nurses, greeted me with a happy smile. In one hand she was waving the medications order sheet for Lena, the six-year-old girl with leukemia. In the other hand Svetlana was holding a filled syringe.

"Who gave you this order?" I asked.

"The professor. Who else?" she responded with a note of surprise in her voice. "He said that the hospital chief signed this order for Lena. Then Svetlana whispered, "Her grandfather is one of the Communist Party leaders."

I was prepared to justify choosing Lena as a recipient of the drug, but I could not justify party favoritism. Their lying and corruption were readily apparent to me.

Even with treatment, Lena succumbed to leukemia as did the other two children. The devastated staff of our pediatric hematology ward contemplated the same questions. What if one of the other two, instead of Lena, had received the treatment? What if we had accurately assessed each of these patients and decided jointly who would be the best candidate for treatment? What if? What if?

Time and time again I felt like everything was my fault. In this case, the life or death of these children depended on me as the treating physician. I carried this burden for many years, until I acknowledged that the system, not I, was to blame—the system, which ensured its own longevity with the complicity of others to remain silent.

In the US many people asked me the same question: "Did you really have any choices when you lived in the USSR?"

"Obviously, not too many choices. Too many questions, though," I always responded. When I was unable to answer these decisive questions—"What is the cost of life? What is the cost of my freedom?"—I felt ready to make a transition, to practice medicine solely on ethical and scientific criteria regardless of the personal or institutional costs.

When I recovered from my surgery, I faced one of the darkest days of my life. Ironically, it was a bright spring day when I was scheduled to start my first chemotherapy treatment. Fearful thoughts pervaded my mind, tore me apart, and brought back images of my little patients who trusted me. I also thought of their parents who believed in me and in the power of the chemotherapy I prescribed.

During my pretreatment orientation, I played the part of a patient, not a doctor who had been practicing oncology for over twenty-five years on both sides of the globe. I listened to the names of the drugs I would be receiving, their doses, and their side effects. By the end of my hour-long meeting, I felt grateful and empathetic. I was no longer thinking only of myself; I felt protective toward other patients who were experiencing similar trauma. Now it was my turn to rebuild trust in medical staff, in spite of being paralyzed with fear and full of uncertainty about the effects and outcome of my prolonged treatment.

"Doctor Shapiro." The nurse's voice was soft and comforting as she greeted me and ushered me in.

"Please call me Alla," I said. "I am just one of the patients who greatly appreciates and respects everything that you're doing for us."

I made myself comfortable in a cozy leather chair, opened my computer, and started writing. By the end of the eight-hour treatment session, I had drafted my first chapters. In these chronicles, I noted how the change in order from doctor-patient to patient-doctor had made a world of difference.

Thanks to skillful physicians, nurses, and staff—and to the chemotherapy medications I received in the right amounts, at the right time—I survived my late radiation-induced cancer. Then I continued with renewed dedication to explore medical countermeasures against damaging incidental and accidental radiation exposure. I was also interested in the possibility of using these medications to protect the healthy tissues of cancer patients undergoing radiation treatment.

CHAPTER 29

Chernobyl

Thirty Years After

To this day, the accident at Chernobyl remains the most serious catastrophe to occur in the nuclear power industry. The approaching thirty-year anniversary triggered a chain of emotional memories of one event after another. I vividly recalled when and where I received the shocking news about the explosion, and I remember the people I worked with, the patients I cared for, and the irrevocable loss of my belief in the words and actions of the Soviet government. The thirty-year commemoration of Chernobyl struck me as the anniversary of a loss.

One spring day in 2016, a colleague and friend, Zhanat Carr, who worked at the World Health Organization (WHO), called me. Skipping the usual polite questions, my friend asked in a firm voice, "Are you going to Germany in June?"

"Why?" I asked in surprise.

She said, "To the 4th International Seminar, 'Radiation Medicine in Research and Practice: Health effects 30 years after Chernobyl, 5 years after Fukushima.' WHO organized the event jointly with the

Medical Biophysical Center in Moscow and the Department of Nuclear Medicine, University Hospital, of Würzburg. The United States is also providing support for this event. It will be interesting for you, and you need some closure," she added.

"How do you know I need closure?" I asked with growing interest.

Surprised by the question, my friend replied: "Have you forgotten how many times you've told me your story?"

Zhanat continued, "Scientists from around the world will discuss numerous radiation-related matters: acute and long-term health effects of radiation after the Chernobyl accident, and the effects of radiation exposure following the damage to four reactors at the Fukushima Daiichi plant in Japan." It had been five years since a magnitude 9.0 earthquake triggered a tsunami off the coast of Japan. A fourteen-meter wave flooded four of six reactors at the power plant on March 11, 2011.

"You are invited to join the discussion on different aspects of radiation's effects, and also to share your experience as a physician first responder."

I did not need more convincing: I was ready to go! All unpleasant emotions attached to my past experience dissipated, and I looked forward to sharing lessons learned at Chernobyl. I was hoping that close attention to the Fukushima Daiichi disaster in Japan and an honest analysis of events would answer many questions, after which I would be ready to move on.

Zhanat Carr and I had met in Kiev at the international conference dedicated to the twentieth anniversary of the Chernobyl disaster. Dr. Carr held the position of medical officer and she represented the WHO Ionizing Radiation Team of the Radiation and

Environmental Health Unit. With her amazing energy, professional and personal skills, and dedication, she was put in charge of coordinating of WHO's activities. She has led meetings in radiation/nuclear accident preparedness and response within the framework of United Nations interagency cooperation; she has coordinated WHO expert groups for research on the health effects of exposure to low doses of ionizing radiation, like those endured by victims of the Chernobyl accident and other accidents involving radioactive materials; and she was involved in developing WHO guidance for occupational cosmic radiation exposure and other environmental radiation health issues.

I arrived in Würzburg on a rainy morning in June. The clouds seemed to disperse as familiar faces brightened my day. We conference participants reminisced about the many previously unknown risks and the trauma we had been exposed to, along with the thousands of victims that we had treated.

Participants from sixteen countries—Australia, Austria, Belarus, Belgium, Croatia, France, Germany, Japan, the Netherlands, Norway, Russia, Sweden, Switzerland, the UK, Ukraine, and the USA—attended the meeting.[49] Along with colleagues whom I had met over the decades at many domestic and international meetings and conferences, I saw some new faces. I considered myself a veteran in the field of radiation, and greatly enjoyed engaging with the curious and restless minds of the new generation of experts in the field.

On the occasion of the thirtieth and the fifth anniversaries of the nuclear accidents, in Chernobyl in 1986, and in Fukushima in 2011, respectively, topics of the two-day seminar focused on the health effects and lessons learned from those accidents. At the opening session, attendees expressed agreement with a strong statement delivered

by one of the presenters in his introduction: "A nuclear accident anywhere has the potential to be a nuclear accident everywhere." This
momentous idea reflects the timeless link between two cataclysmic
events that occurred twenty-five years apart: the nuclear explosion at
the Chernobyl power station and the triple disaster in Fukushima.

Throughout the presentations, we revisited the events of the night
of April 26, 1986: the powerful explosion and fire, the firefighters who
succumbed to slow death, and the uncontrolled radioactive release into
the atmosphere and, downwind, to areas around the world. The silence
in the audience eloquently expressed their emotions. World experts in
radiation emphasized the major role of dosimetry, that is, methods of
quantifying the dose of radiation received by individuals, and I could
not resist commenting on the obvious and pivotal importance of accurate measurements.

"I agree that knowing the dose of radiation is extremely important. Dosimeters would really help, but only if the numbers are not
'adjusted' (recalibrated) to provide desired readings, which is what
happened at Chernobyl."

One of my former colleagues from Russia, Professor Andrey
Bushmanov, backed up my assertion. Andrey and I had shared
decades of collaboration on common objectives: to strengthen radiation emergency preparedness and to boost research on the health
consequences associated with radiation exposure. Dr. Bushmanov
has had a distinguished career, starting as a physician at the Hospital
No. 6 in Moscow. He was eventually appointed to the position of
professor and first deputy director at the Federal Medical-Biological
Agency of Russia.

Another respondent recalled that peasants bribed officials to
lower the numbers that reflected high levels of radiation in fruits and

berries to make them "clear for sale." Yet another participant made an even more eye-opening statement—that the levels of radiation in Kiev were presented falsely as lower than they really were in order to delay evacuation of children from the city.

Our memories from Chernobyl were still fresh. In a special ceremony, we commemorated the emergency response personnel who gave their lives to protect others, and we mourned patients who did not survive their injuries. I shared a photo of the Kiev monument dedicated "to those who died."

Thirty years after the explosion, much of the broader area around Chernobyl is still unsafe. It remains a chilling reminder of nuclear disaster: radiation levels around the plant remain so high that authorities do not expect the area to be inhabitable for between 180 and 320 years. The town of Pripyat is surrounded by forests, which, according to some studies, now teem with wildlife because so few humans have dared to enter them.

Scientific data have helped to shape our understanding of how to improve existing approaches and develop new prophylactic and treatment measures against radiation exposure. In efforts to create better control and management of potential nuclear disasters, I continue to share the findings of my Ukrainian counterparts with my American colleagues.

Lessons learned from the Chernobyl accident in Ukraine informed the emergency response that followed Fukushima. For instance, instead of taking days to evacuate (as was the case in Chernobyl), residents from the area surrounding the Fukushima Daiichi plant were promptly evacuated. There were no radiation casualties (from acute radiation syndrome) following the disaster. However, forty-six employees of the Fukushima station and twenty-one contractors received a dose of more than 100 mSv, the level at which there is an acknowledged slight increase in cancer risk later in life. Experts agree that there probably will not be a detectable rise in thyroid cancer or leukemia, the two cancers most likely to result from such an accident.[50] The risk to the roughly 140,000 civilians who had been living within a few tens of kilometers of the plant seems even lower. At most, residents of Fukushima received less than a 10 mSv dose of radiation, which is a typical dose for one abdominal computed tomography (CT) scan.

A far greater health risk may have resulted from the psychological stress of the event. An emotional effect similar to that observed after Chernobyl has been reported in the aftermath of the Fukushima disaster. The study conducted to monitor the mental health status of evacuees found that evacuation and relocation of large groups of people led to widespread post-traumatic stress disorder (PTSD). It should be noted that many people who lost their homes and jobs were placed in temporary housing in shelters and did not have adequate access to health care.

Additionally, many deaths, especially of elderly evacuees, were attributed to repeated evacuations from one place to another, and limited access to medical intervention or critical supportive care. The human cost of evacuation was chilling. Dr. Sae Ochi, a physician at the Japan Agency for Medical Research and Development who has worked in Fukushima, shared the following statistics: "If you compare nursing homes that evacuated with those that didn't, the death rate was three times higher among those who moved; of the disaster-related deaths, 1,984 were people over the age of 65."[51]

The distressing discovery of these similarities, thirty years after Chernobyl and five years after the Fukushima disasters, proves that both visible and invisible wounds are constants in nuclear catastrophes. The symposium in Würzburg did bring a sense of closure to me and helped to heal some of my hidden wounds.[52]

CHAPTER 30

Health Effects of the Chernobyl Accident

Within three months after the Chernobyl disaster, twenty-seven first responders died from direct exposure to radiation. Those who were evacuated and the general population suffered from cancer, heart diseases, and other complications associated with radiation exposure.

Acute radiation sickness (ARS) was considered first in 237 victims, but actually confirmed in 134 people. The initial much-larger number reflects the fact that medical personnel, lacking adequate knowledge of radiation, were not familiar with the sickness and how it progresses.[53] ARS occurs when the whole body, or significant portions of the body, receive more than 1 Gy (Gy is a unit of radiation). Subsyndromes of ARS include damage to the bone marrow, the skin, the gastrointestinal system, the brain, and the heart. Diagnosis and selection of treatments depend on the presence of symptoms, their severity, and their time of occurrence.

Dedicated doctors and nurses spent endless days and nights trying to apply sparse information about radiation damage to patients. Physicists helped to reconstruct the radiation dose that each patient had been exposed to. Alas, efforts to expeditiously measure radioactivity in biological specimens, such as blood, urine, feces, or sweat, failed because we did not have needed equipment and we were unprepared to respond to mass casualties. Our medical system was overwhelmed.

It should be noted that computerized approaches to assessing the degree of exposure to radiation did not exist in the former Soviet Union in the late 1980s. At the time, doctors relied on clinical information on each victim, as well as patients' responses to questionnaires. In addition, frequently changing opinions, messages, and instructions delayed the processing of blood and tissue samples.

Despite aggressive treatments, twenty-seven workers from the nuclear power station died in the first days and weeks and up to three months after exposure to very high doses of radiation. In addition to bone marrow failure, almost every patient had radiation injury to more than one organ or system.

A few weeks after the disaster, a world-renowned expert on bone marrow transplantation from the Unites States reached out to the Soviet president, Mikhail Gorbachev. The Communist Party leader asked the physician to come "immediately" to Moscow and Kiev, which he did, bearing suitcases filled with syringes, needles, tubes for intravenous injections, masks, and rubber gloves. These gifts reflected the sympathetic response from the international community.

The hospital in Moscow was finally prepared to take care of patients, mostly firefighters and first responders, who required bone marrow transplants. The procedure was performed on thirteen patients. However, all of these patients died, except one individual whose body rejected the transplant but recovered its own marrow. The outcome shocked everyone who relied on this procedure as a last resort and their last hope to save the lives of these heroes. For years some colleagues in the US and Russia and family members of the deceased blamed the American doctor for the failure of the procedure.

In hindsight, we realized that the patients who died after the bone marrow transplants actually succumbed to combined injuries, such as ARS and extensive thermal (caused by fires) and radiation burns. In fact, radiation burns were the main cause of death for the majority of patients.[54] Otherwise, the bone marrow transplants might have saved their lives.

Committees around the world have performed comprehensive analyses of the early and delayed (or long-term) effects of radiation exposure. Although cleanup workers had increased risk of developing different forms of leukemia, the main causes of death in this group were cancer and cardiovascular disease. For exposed children and adolescents, delayed health effects included an unprecedented increase in thyroid cancer, starting six years after the accident. Treatment involves surgical removal of the thyroid gland.[55]

Even though the strong connection between thyroid cancer and the release of radioactive iodine had already been established, in the first few weeks after the accident, controls on contaminated food were not implemented in the USSR, so that people, the majority of them children, consumed milk with high radioactive iodine-131 concentrations.

The results for childhood leukemia are inconclusive and remain a subject for future analysis. Controversy surrounds data on the incidence of leukemia in children exposed in utero. In some studies of the incidence of childhood leukemia, thyroid cancer, and diseases in first responders and cleanup workers, statistical analysis failed

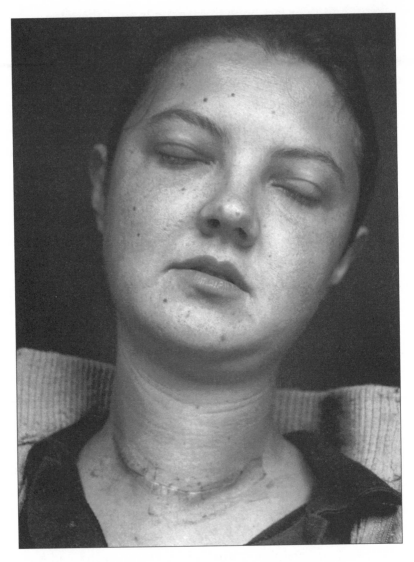

FIG. 21. Starting six years after the Chernobyl accident, there was an unprecedented increase in thyroid cancer among children. The horizontal scar left on the base of the neck after surgery to remove cancerous thyroid glands acquired the name "Chernobyl necklace." *Photograph courtesy of Gabriela Bulisova.*

because it did not distinguish the groups of interest from the general population. Age and gender seem to be an important consideration for proper analysis, but in many studies, these factors were not taken into account.

The high rate of thyroid cancer that was reported may be attributed to the increased screening of the local population that took place after the Chernobyl accident. Either during routine medical visits or during exams for some other condition, there were more frequent neck examinations. Approximately forty percent of the reported thyroid cancer cases were found through screening programs, and it is unclear how many of these cancers would otherwise have gone undetected.[56]

CHAPTER 31

Fire and Deception

On Sunday, April 5, 2020, one of my friends living in the US sent me a text message. I had known the sender, Anna, for many years; we worked together for a long time in the radiation health effects field and attended many domestic and international conferences together. My friend is a brilliant and dedicated physician and researcher who keeps abreast of issues regarding Chernobyl, past and current. Anna's text message began with these words: "News story about fire near Chernobyl now." I quickly scrolled down the short page and concluded that I needed more details. Therefore, I searched for reliable information online. Words such as "burning woods, deadly radioactive elements, grass, ferns, and environmental impact" reappeared from the past. *Would they ever disappear from my memory?* I wondered.

The blaze started on Friday, April 3, near the site of the world's worst nuclear disaster, and spread to nearby forests. The fires came after unusually dry weather, but police also reported that a twenty-seven-year old local resident deliberately set fire to grass in the region. Ukrainian authorities attempted to play down fears that the radiation could spread to the capital, Kiev, just sixty-two miles from

Pripyat. The three other reactors at Chernobyl had continued to generate electricity until the power station finally closed in 2000. In 2016 a giant protective dome was put in place over the fourth reactor.

As happened thirty-five years ago, rumors spread quickly. Authorities became aware that radiation levels over the weekend had soared to sixteen times higher than usual. However, the citizens of the surrounding areas, including Kiev, the capital of Ukraine, were kept in the dark.[57] Three days after the fire started, I called my friends in Kiev to find out what they knew of forest fires near the site of the Chernobyl nuclear disaster. They had not heard about it. "There are no open flames," the state emergency service said in a statement on Tuesday morning, April 7. There was still a "slight smoldering of the forest floor," the agency added, noting that more than four hundred firefighters and other personnel were still working in the area.[58]

Finally, on Tuesday, April 14, the heroic efforts of the deployed crews and rainy weather extinguished the flames in Chernobyl's exclusion zone, leaving burned trees and grass, and wild horses fleeing across scorched earth. The first spring flowers withered. Emerald Camp, a popular tourist location, had burned to the ground.

The announcement about the Chernobyl nuclear disaster thirty-five years ago first came to my attention via the radio station Voice of America. Now the dire news of the Chernobyl fires was delivered to my Kiev friends via my voice from America. I told them that firefighters were working hard to extinguish the fire, that the level of radiation in that area significantly exceeded the normal level.

Thirty-five years later, disinformation continues to be sent from the top to the bottom of the political ladder, even though history has revealed that lies negatively impact everyone working in response to a disaster. If public officials fail to communicate with citizens about what's going on inside a country during a crisis, then they cannot help themselves, and help from outside will not reach them. Apparently, some lessons remain unlearned.

CHAPTER 32

Echoes of Chernobyl

America's Preparedness Failure

Fortune favors the prepared mind.

—Louis Pasteur

T hirty-four years after the Chernobyl accident, the novel coronavirus has changed our world. Designated government agencies were supposed to take timely action in responding to the pandemic and protecting the country and its citizens. The failure of these efforts is reminiscent of the Chernobyl disaster.

In February 2020, the coronavirus (COVID-19) outbreak in China became a pandemic.[59] It shuttered country after country, and no continent eluded its grasp. The streets of the French capital were empty, and the always-illuminated Eiffel Tower grew dark. New York City's subway system stopped running around the clock, and there were no more daytime adventures or midnight carriage rides in Central Park. Supportive hugs are now potentially lethal, and affection for family and friends must be expressed at a "social distance."

In response to the pandemic, the Strategic National Stockpile (SNS) began deployment to areas in need of personal protective equipment (PPE), including N95 respirators, surgical and face masks, face shields, gloves, and disposable gowns, to help prevent COVID-19 transmission. To my surprise, the initial distribution did not last long. As the infection rate soared, hospitals stopped receiving the supplies they needed. President Donald Trump blamed this on the SNS, claiming, "We took over an empty shelf. We took over a very depleted place, in a lot of ways."[60]

This statement did not entirely jibe with my personal experience of the SNS nor with my knowledge of recent efforts to bolster the SNS. In 2002 I participated in the SNS Radiation Working Group, convened by the Centers for Disease Control and Prevention (CDC). The group comprised radiation experts from the US government and academia, including a world-class leader in the medical management of radiation injuries, Professor Nicholas Dainiak, MD, director of the Department of Therapeutic Radiology at Yale University School of Medicine. Our group developed guidelines for evaluating and managing large-scale incidents in which thousands or tens of thousands of persons would be exposed to radiation. We also recommended that medications be stockpiled at undisclosed locations for use in a mass-casualty nuclear incident. In case of a loss of infrastructure, these assets were to be delivered as "push packages" anywhere in the United States or its territories within twelve hours of a federal decision to deploy them.[61]

These recommendations were turned over to the CDC and to the Health and Human Services (HHS) assistant secretary for preparedness and response (ASPR). The latter leads the nation's medical and public health preparedness programs for public health emergencies such as pandemics, as well as terrorist incidents involving the use of radiological, chemical, or biological materials.

In addition to the CDC and the HHS, the FDA and other federal agencies work every day to help prepare the nation for potential threats. I am most familiar with the intensive research being done to develop medical countermeasures (MCMs) that can be used to prevent or treat damage that results from exposure to high doses of radiation. Some of these FDA-approved countermeasures have been added to the stockpile and are currently available for rapid and safe use in catastrophic nuclear or radiological events.[62]

The Strategic National Stockpile was created in 2003 as a successor to a less extensive government stockpiling program. In 2006 the Pandemic and All-Hazards Preparedness Act (PAHPA) passed, and it was reauthorized in 2013, establishing a system that prepared for, and responded to, public health threats. That system included funding for the SNS.

Since its establishment, the SNS has responded to multiple large-scale emergencies. The H1N1 influenza pandemic of 2009 triggered the then-largest deployment in the history of the Strategic National Stockpile. The SNS distributed 85 million N95 respirators—fitted face masks that block most airborne particles—along with millions of other masks, gowns, and gloves. In 2017 the CDC, via the SNS, responded to four disasters—the Zika virus epidemic, and the hurricanes Harvey, Irma, and Maria. The SNS deployed temporary non-acute medical care facilities and caches of medical supplies and equipment.

Although the SNS responded well in these emergencies, it has not always been adequately funded. Between 2003 and 2015, ten government reports predicted that the United States would experience a critical lack of ventilators and other lifesaving medical supplies if it faced a viral outbreak like the one currently sweeping the country.[63]

Congress considered reauthorization of PAHPA in January of 2018, knowing that the prior authorization would expire on October 1 of that year. Witnesses at a Senate hearing shared their concerns about the decreased federal funding, or lack of funding, for preparedness and response.[64] Almost nine months after expiration of the prior authorization, on June 24, 2019, Congress finally passed, and President Trump signed, a reauthorization of PAHPA, known as the Pandemic and All-Hazards Preparedness and Advancing Innovation Act (PAHPAI). However, Congress appropriated far less money for the bill than public health experts recommended.[65]

Funding for the stockpile hovered around $600 million per year from 2016 to 2018. Congress boosted that amount to just over $700 million in 2019. Yet reports in 2019 from the agency in charge of maintaining the stockpile warned that more than a billion dollars would be needed to replenish its stores and replace expired drugs and equipment.[66]

It seems that lack of funding was not the only reason for the rapid depletion of the stockpile and the government's general lack of preparedness. A range of contributing factors came to light during a simulated-pandemic exercise that the HHS conducted from January to August 2019. "Crimson Contagion," as it was called, assumed that the pandemic originated in China and resulted in over 500,000 deaths in the US. These were the findings of the exercise as set forth in a draft report in October 2019 (as far as I know a final report has not been issued):

- The federal government lacked sufficient funding to respond to a severe influenza pandemic.

- Exercise participants lacked clarity on the roles of different federal agencies.
- HHS had difficulties providing accurate and relevant information to hospitals and other public health organizations.
- There was confusion between the HHS, FEMA, and the Department of Homeland Security on which federal agency would take the lead in the crisis.
- The US lacked the production capacity to meet the demands imposed by a pandemic for protective equipment and medical devices such as masks and ventilators.
- States were unable to efficiently request resources due to the lack of a standardized request process.[67]

A *New York Times* article reiterated the claim that the "Crimson Contagion" simulation revealed confusion about who was in charge and what kind of equipment was available. The article also reported that cities and states acted on their own, and the federal government failed to lead, "leaving the nation with funding shortfalls, equipment shortages and disorganization within and among various branches and levels of government."[68]

In 2020 dire predictions were borne out as the COVID-19 virus spread across the US. Underfunded and understaffed state and local health care facilities were swiftly overwhelmed. They scrambled to ramp up testing, investigate virus hotspots, and obtain desperately needed protective equipment for health care workers. In the absence of a coordinated federal plan to procure and distribute ventilators, masks, and other medical equipment, governors bid against each other for that gear on the open market, pleading with corporations for donations, and encouraging medical personnel to craft their own homemade supplies.

In 1986 the Soviet Union mishandled the Chernobyl nuclear explosion, in part because that country did not know how to prepare for such a disaster. In contrast, the US knew how to prepare for a pandemic, but did not do it. Though President Trump insisted that the Obama administration left him with a bare cupboard, it is apparent that many failures occurred under his watch. Calls for action during hearings and legislation in 2018 and 2019 were not heeded. Nor were measures taken to rectify the problems revealed by the 2019 Crimson Contagion exercise.

Here is my "prescription" for change in our country: improve governmental transparency and government oversight, institute discreet budgeting for disaster preparedness, improve government agency coordination, partner with other nations on disaster preparedness efforts, and reinstate US membership in the World Health Organization and other international disaster preparedness groups.

EPILOGUE

Preparing for the Next Disaster

On April 26, 1986, a radiation plume from the exploded unit at the Chernobyl nuclear power station spread over Ukraine, Belarus, and many parts of Europe. My fellow Soviet citizens and I woke up in a different world, and were totally unprepared to live in it. The disaster was compounded by the Soviet government's lack of preparation and subsequent failure to provide a proper response to the explosion.

Government officials withheld timely and truthful information from the public and from first responders, including physicians. They initially denied that there had been a radiation accident and claimed that reports of dangerous levels of radiation were rumors. Egregiously, the Soviet government did not share facts and details with the international professional community. At the time of the catastrophe, the USSR had no comprehensive strategy for assessing and managing health effects from radiation on different population age groups. The psychological effects, such as depression, anxiety, and suicide, were even worse than the physical illnesses, such as cancer and radiation burns or poisoning.

After witnessing the potential self-destruction of the human race by nuclear power, along with Soviet deception about it, and after enduring anti-Semitism for generations, my family finally left the Soviet Union in 1989. We were among the "stateless" Jewish refugees—without citizenship in any country. Our emigration journey lasted six months.

When I was living safely in the US, I looked back at my experiences as a Chernobyl first responder and as a Jewish refugee, and I thought, *Life is not only precious but precarious.* At any moment, the heavens could pour down rain and drown us, the earth could open up and swallow us, and myriad man-made weapons and practices could render the planet uninhabitable.

Motivated by first-hand experience, I embraced a career path that took me deep into the development of new drugs for the prevention and treatment of radiation injuries in humans. I participated in multiple simulated exercises, conducted by US government agencies, to coordinate responses to radiation emergencies, such as terrorist "dirty bombs," nuclear attacks, and radiation accidents. Currently, there are ninety-nine nuclear reactors in thirty American states, and there could be an accidental release of radiation from any of these facilities.

The tendency to believe that a cataclysmic event, such as a nuclear explosion or a pandemic, won't happen to us again is known as "disaster amnesia." If we deny the possibility of future disasters, then history will repeat itself in an endless loop—new unthinkable and unpredictable disasters will happen again and again until we replace disaster amnesia with crisis retrospection.

In mid-February of 2020, the novel coronavirus began to reshape daily life across the world. As with Chernobyl, the pandemic uncovered a lack of preparedness in the US, and there was much conflicting information about the virus and how to protect against it. The government failed to keep its citizens up to date with timely, reliable information based on science, not on fear. Hundreds of thousands of citizens sought care from an overwhelmed medical system. Long-standing systemic health, economic, and social inequities put many people from racial and ethnic minority groups at increased risk of getting sick and dying from COVID-19.

Among the hardest psychological challenges of this pandemic has been social isolation. Public health requirements, such as social distancing, can make people feel lonely and can increase stress and anxiety—even for those who are trained to withstand isolation, such as astronauts. On April 16, 2020, a crew of three American astronauts who had been in space for many months returned to a starkly different planet. Their Soyuz capsule landed in Kazakhstan, which had declared a state of emergency, and most of the airports were closed. One of the astronauts said, "It will be difficult to not give hugs to family and friends after being up here for seven months. I think I will feel more isolated on Earth than in space."[69]

There are lessons to be learned from the Chernobyl disaster and the COVID-19 pandemic. Governments should keep citizens informed of dangers, whether radiation exposure or a virulent virus, so that protective measures can be taken. They should provide access to relevant scientific knowledge and data, lest fear and pseudoscientific facts take their place. They should treat their citizens equitably so that they do not become demoralized and lose respect for government institutions. Finally, governments must develop a national strategy for dealing with catastrophes, and they must ensure good coordination among all levels of government and all government agencies as they prepare—without denial of science, and without delay—for the next disaster.

NOTES

1   The name of my workplace changed as follows: 2001–2002, Division of Counter-Terrorism; 2002–2004, Office of Counter-Terrorism; 2004–2014, Office of Counter-Terrorism and Emergency Coordination (OCTEC); and 2014–present Counter-Terrorism and Emergency Coordination Staff (CTECS).

2   Robert Mcconnell, "Remembering the Soviet Response to Chernobyl," *National Review*, April 26, 2011, http://www. nationalreview.com/corner/265612.

3   US Food and Drug Administration website, Bioterrorism and Drug Preparedness, "Frequently Asked Questions on Potassium Iodide (KI)," https://www.fda.gov/drugs/ bioterrorism-and-drug-preparedness/frequently-asked-questions-potassium-iodide-ki.

4   R. F. Mould, *Chernobyl Record: The Definitive History of the Chernobyl Catastrophe* (Boca Raton, FL: CRC Press, 2000).

5   H. Viinamaki, E. Kumpusalo, M. Myllykangas, S. Salomaa, L. Kumpusalo, S. Kolmakov, I. Ilchenko, G. Zhukowsky, and A. Nissinen, "The Chernobyl Accident and Mental Wellbeing: A Population Study," *Acta Psychiatrica Scandinavica* 91, no. 6 (1995): 396–401.

6   Kaja Rahu, Mati Rahu, Mare Tekkel, and Evelyn Bromet, "Sui-
     cide Risk among Chernobyl Cleanup Workers in Estonia Still
     Increased: An Updated Cohort Study," *Annals of Epidemiology*
     16, no.12 (2006): 917–919, doi:10.1016/j.annepidem.2006.07.006.

7   Konstantin N. Loganovsky and Tatiana K. Loganovskaja, "At
     Issue: Schizophrenia Spectrum Disorders in Persons Exposed
     to Ionizing Radiation as a Result of the Chernobyl Accident,"
     Schizophrenia Bulletin 26, no. 4 (2000): 751–773.

8   World Health Organization, "1986–2016: Chernobyl at 30,"
     April 25, 2016, https://www.who.int/who-documents-
     detail/1986-2016-chernobyl-at-30.

9   "Excerpts from Gorbachev's Speech on Chernobyl Accident,"
     New York Times, May 15, 1986, http://www.nytimes.
     com/1986/05/15/world/excerpts-from-gorbachev-s-speech-
     on-chernobyl-accident.html?pagewanted=all.

10   International Nuclear Safety Advisory Group, International Atomic
     Energy Agency, "INSAG-7, The Chernobyl Accident: Updating of
     INSAG-1," Safety Series No. 75-INSAG-7, 1992, http://www-pub.
     iaea.org/MTCD/publications/PDF/Pub913e_web.pdf.

11   National Institutes of Health, US National Library of Medicine,
     ClinicalTrials.gov, BIO 300 Non-Small Cell Lung Cancer Study
     (NSCLC), https://clinicaltrials.gov/ct2/show/
     NCT02567799?term=BIO+300&cond=Lung+Cancer&cn-
     try=US&draw=2&rank=1.

12   World Health Organization, "Health Effects of the Chernobyl Accident and Special Health Care Programmes," Geneva, 2006, https://www.who.int/ionizing_radiation/chernobyl/WHO%20 Report%20on%20Chernobyl%20Health%20Effects%20 July%2006.pdf.

13   David R. *Marples, Ukraine under Perestroika: Ecology, Economics and the Workers' Revolt* (Edmonton: University of Alberta Press, 1991).

14   University of Pittsburgh Schools of the Health Sciences, "Plant Antioxidant May Protect Against Radiation Exposure," ScienceDaily, 24 September 2008, https://www.winespectator. com/articles/red-wine-compound-may-protect-against-effects-of-radiation-poisoning-4375.

15   Heng Zhang, Hao Yan, Xiaoliang Zhou, Huaqing Wang, Yiling Yang, Junling Zhang, and Hui Wang, "The Protective Effects of Resveratrol Against Radiation-Induced Intestinal Injury," *BMC Complementary and Alternative Medicine* 17, no. 410 (2017), https://doi.org/10.1186/s12906-017-1915-9.

16   Shannon Reagan-Shaw, Hasan Mukhtar, and Nihal Ahmad, "Resveratrol Imparts Photoprotection of Normal Cells and Enhances the Efficacy of Radiation Therapy in Cancer Cells," *Photochemistry and Photobiology*, January 23, 2008, https:// onlinelibrary.wiley.com/doi/full/10.1111/j.1751-1097.2007.00279.x

17 United States Holocaust Museum, *Holocaust Encyclopedia*, s.v. "Kiev and Babi Yar," https://encyclopedia.ushmm.org/content/en/article/kiev-and-babi-yar.

18 Mark A. Clarfield, "The Soviet 'Doctors' Plot'—50 Years On," *British Medical Journal* 325, no. 7378 (2002): 1487–1489.

19 Robin Munro, "Dangerous Minds: Political Psychiatry in China Today and its Origins in the Mao Era," Human Rights Watch, Geneva Initiative on Psychiatry, 2002, https://www.hrw.org/reports/2002/china02/.

20 Carl M. Kjellstrand, "History of Dialysis. Men and Ideas," online lecture for Nordic Nephrology Days, University of Lund Selected Symposia, May 1997, http://www.hdcn.com/symp/lund/kjel.htm.

21 Adam Kirsch, "Stefan Zweig and Joseph Roth: How Europe's Exiled Intellectuals Ended up on a Belgian Beach," *The New Statesman*, January 25, 2016, http://www.newstatesman.com/culture/books/2016/01/stefan-zweig-and-joseph-roth-how-europe-s-exiled-intellectuals-ended-belgian.

22 Eleanor Brown, *The Weird Sisters* (Detroit, MI: Amy Einhorn Books/Putnam, 2011).

23 Melissa Healy, "U.S. Will Review Status of 4,200 Soviet Jews: INS Ordered to Reopen Cases of Applicants Denied Admission as Refugees," *Los Angeles Times*, September 15, 1989,

http://articles.latimes.com/1989-09-15/news/
mn-173_1_soviet-union.

24   Vici.org, "Baths of Caracalla," https://vici.org/vici/7894/#:~:-
     text=The%20Baths%20of%20Caracalla%20(Italian,in%20
     the%20lifetime%20of%20Caracalla.

25   Fred A. Lazin, "Refugee Resettlement and 'Freedom of Choice':
     The Case of Soviet Jewry," July 1, 2005, https://cis.org/Report/
     Refugee-Resettlement-and-Freedom-Choice-Case-Soviet-Jewry.

26   peoplepill.com, Oleksandr Anatoliyovych Zavarov biography,
     https://upclosed.com/people/oleksandr-zavarov/.

27   Dmitry Babich, "Ukrainian Soccer Legends Receive Call to
     Arms—Against Their Will," Sputnik International website,
     2015, https://sputniknews.com/
     columnists/201502161018353466/.

28   The Criterion Collection, "'Ti amo': An Exchange of Letters,"
     October 4, 2013, https://www.criterion.com/current/
     posts/2922--ti-amo-an-exchange-of-letters.

29   Council on Hemispheric Affairs, "Cuba—Russia Now and
     Then," February 24, 2010, http://www.coha.org/cuba-russia-now-
     and-then/.

30   American Battle Monuments Commission, "World War II
     Strategic Bombing Campaign Online Interactive Released,"

January 6, 2015, www.abms.gov/news-events/news/
world-war-ii-strategic-bombing-campaign.

31 atomicarchive.com, Khrushchev to Kennedy, October 24,
    1962, https://www.atomicarchive.com/resources/documents/
    cuba/khrushchev-letter-1.html.

32 John F. Kennedy Presidential Library and Museum, "Cuban
    Missile Crisis," https://www.jfklibrary.org/JFK/JFK-in-History/
    Cuban-Missile-Crisis.aspx.

33 William D. Montalbano, "Italian Resort Finds Itself Swamped
    by Flood of Soviet Emigres," *Los Angeles Times*, February 19,
    1989, https://www.latimes.com/archives/la-xpm-1989-02-19-
    mn-420-story.html.

34 Ariel Roguin, "Rene Theophile Hyacinthe Laënnec (1781–
    1826): The Man Behind the Stethoscope," *Clinical Medicine &
    Research* 4, no. 3 (2006): 230–235, doi:10.3121/cmr.4.3.230.

35 The V device, worn on the Army Commendation Medal and
    other awards, stands for "valor." The device was authorized
    decades ago for wear on US Army ribbons. According to *Wiki-
    pedia*, "The Purple Heart is a United States military decoration
    awarded in the name of the President to those wounded or
    killed while serving, on or after April 5, 1917, with the U.S.
    military. With its forerunner, the Badge of Military Merit, which
    took the form of a heart made of purple cloth, the Purple Heart
    is the oldest military award still given to U.S. military members."

36   Now called Chernobyl Children International, the organiza-
     tion has since provided humanitarian aid to the children of
     Ukraine, Belarus, and Western Russia affected by radiation
     from the Chernobyl accident.

37   A. H. Wu, M. C. Yu, C-C. Tseng, and M. C. Pike, "Epidemiol-
     ogy of Soy Exposures and Breast Cancer Risk," *British Journal
     of Cancer* 98 (2008): 9–14, https://doi.org/10.1038/
     sj.bjc.6604145.

38   Chris H. Takimoto et al., "Phase I Pharmacokinetic and Phar-
     macodynamic Analysis of Unconjugated Soy Isoflavones
     Administered to Individuals with Cancer," *Cancer Epidemiol-
     ogy, Biomarkers & Prevention* 12 (November 2003): 1213–
     1221, https://cebp.aacrjournals.org/content/cebp/12/11/1213.
     full.pdf.

39   Stephen Barnes, "The Chemopreventive Properties of Soy
     Isoflavonoids in Animal Models of Breast Cancer," *Breast
     Cancer Research and Treatment* 46 (1997): 169–179, https://
     link.springer.com/article/10.1023/A:1005956326155.

40   Justia Patents, Patents by Inventor Alla Shapiro, https://patents.
     justia.com/inventor/alla-shapiro.

41   Justia Patents, "Phytoestrogenic isoflavone compositions, their
     preparation and use thereof for protection against and treat-
     ment of radiation injury, https://patents.justia.com/
     patent/7655694.

42 Michael R. Landauer, Adam J. Harvey, Michael D. Kaytor, and
Regina M. Day, "Mechanism and Therapeutic Window of a
Genistein Nanosuspension to Protect against Hematopoietic-
Acute Radiation Syndrome," *Journal of Radiation Research* 60,
no. 3 (May 2019): 308–317, https://academic.oup.com/jrr/
article/60/3/308/5481946.

43 Humanetics Pharmaceuticals, "Humanetics Corporation to
Present at the Annual Meeting of the American Society for
Radiation Oncology," news release, October 23, 2018, https://
www.humaneticscorp.com/october-23-2018.

44 National Institutes of Health, US National Library of Medicine,
ClinicalTrails.gov, "Bio 300 Non-Small Cell Lung Cancer Study
(NSCLC)," https://clinicaltrials.gov/ct2/show/NCT02567799.

45 MCM is an FDA-wide initiative to coordinate medical
countermeasure (MCM) development in the event of a potential public health emergency stemming from a terrorist's attack
with biological, chemical, or radiological/nuclear material.

46 Food and Drug Administration, "What Are Medical Countermeasures? https://www.fda.gov/emergency-preparedness-and-
response/about-mcmi/what-are-medical-countermeasures.

47 Food and Drug Administration website, What We Do, https://
www.fda.gov/about-fda/what-we-do.

48   US Department of Health and Human Services, Radiation
     Emergency Medical Management (REMM), Strategic National
     Stockpile, https://www.remm.nlm.gov/sns.htm.

49   World Health Organization, Collaborating Centres, Case
     Studies, Scientific Exchange on Radiation Medicine, https://
     www.who.int/collaboratingcentres/casestudies/en/index6.html.

50   Angelina K. Guskova et al., "Acute Effects of Radiation Expo-
     sure Following the Chernobyl Accident," in *Treatment of
     Radiation Injuries*, ed. Doris Brown (Springer US, 1990), pp
     195–209.

51   Robin Hardig, "Fukushima Nuclear Disaster: Did the Evacua-
     tion Raise the Death Toll?" *Financial Times*, March 2018,
     https://www.ft.com/content/000f864e-22ba-11e8-add1-
     0e8958b189ea. Also see T. Sawano, Y. Nishikawa, A. Ozaki, et
     al., "Premature death associated with long-term evacuation
     among a vulnerable population after the Fukushima nuclear
     disaster: A case report, *Medicine* 98, no. 27 (2019): e16162,
     doi:10.1097/MD.0000000000016162.

52   Geoff Brumfiel, Ichiko Fuyuno, "Japan's Nuclear Crisis: Fukushi-
     ma's Legacy of Fear," *Nature* 483 (March 7, 2012): 138–140.

53   Fred A. Mettler Jr., Angelina K. Gus'kova, Igor Gusev, "Health
     Effects in Those with Acute Radiation Sickness from the
     Chernobyl Accident," *Health Physics* 93, no. 5 (2007): 462–469,
     doi: 10.1097/01.HP.0000278843.27969.74.

54   Nuclear Energy Institute (NEI), "Chernobyl Accident and Its
     Consequences," fact sheet, https://www.nei.org/resources/
     fact-sheets/chernobyl-accident-and-its-consequences.

55   E. Cardis and M. Hatch, "The Chernobyl Accident—An
     Epidemiological Perspective," *Clinical Oncology* 23, no. 4
     (2011): 251–260, doi:10.1016/j.clon.2011.01.510.

56   World Health Organization, "Health Effects of the Chernobyl
     Accident and Special Health Care Programmes," Report of the
     UN Chernobyl Forum Expert Group "Health," 2006, https://
     www.who.int/ionizing_radiation/chernobyl/WHO%20
     Report%20on%20Chernobyl%20Health%20Effects%20
     July%2006.pdf.

57   Andrew Roth, "'Bad News': Radiation 16 Times above Normal
     After Forest Fire Near Chernobyl," *The Guardian*, April 5,
     2020, https://www.theguardian.com/environment/2020/
     apr/06/bad-news-radiation-spikes-16-times-above-normal-
     after-forest-fire-near-chernobyl.

58   Чернобыль в огне: Что происходит в охваченной пожаром
     зоне отчуждения. Хронология событий с первого дня
     пожара. Страшные следы стихии в фото и видео [Chernobyl
     on Fire: What Happens in the Fire-Razor Exclusion Zone.
     Chronology of events from the first day of the fire. Scary traces
     of the elements in photos and videos], April 13, 2020, https://
     112.ua/glavnye-novosti/vtoraya-tragediya-chto-seychas-
     proishodit-v-ohvachennom-ognem-chernobyle-532775.html.

59   After the declaration of a national emergency concerning the
     novel coronavirus disease outbreak was issued in March 2020,
     people started comparing the coronavirus pandemic with the
     Chernobyl disaster. Suddenly, a September 2019 YouTube
     interview with me, "Doctor Fact Checks the HBO Chernobyl
     Series," attracted dramatically increased attention, and as of
     September 2020, it had been viewed by over six million people.
     The video appears on the *Vanity Fair* YouTube channel
     launched by Condé Nast *Entertainment*, at https://youtube.
     com/watch?v=m1GEPsSvpZ7.

60   D'Angelo Gore, FactCheck.org, April 3, 2020, "Trump Falsely
     Claims He Inherited 'Empty' Stockpile," https://www.factcheck.
     org/2020/04/trump-falsely-claims-he-inherited-empty-
     stockpile/.

61   Jamie K. Waselenko, et al., "Medical Management of the Acute
     Radiation Syndrome: Recommendations of the Strategic
     National Stockpile Radiation Working Group, June 15, 2004,
     https://www.acpjournals.org/doi/10.7326/0003-4819-
     140-12-200406150-00015.

62   Vijay K. Singh, Patricia L. P. Romaine, and Thomas M. Seed,
     "Medical Countermeasures for Radiation Exposure and
     Related Injuries: Characterization of Medicines, FDA-Ap-
     proval Status and Inclusion into the Strategic National Stock-
     pile," *Health Physics* 108, no. 6 (June 2015): 607–630,
     doi:10.1097/HP.0000000000000279.

63 Majlie de Puy Kamp, "Federal Officials Repeatedly Warned that US Hospitals Lacked Enough Ventilators," CNN Investigates, March 27, 2020, https://www.cnn.com/2020/03/27/cnn10/ventilators-supply-government-warnings-coronavirus-invs/index.html.

64 Kim Riley, "PAHPA Hearing Witnesses Question U.S. Government's Preparedness, Response Commitment," *Homeland Preparedness News*, January 24, 2018, https://homelandprepnews.com/countermeasures/26388-pahpa-hearing-witnesses-question-u-s-governments-preparedness-response-commitment/.

65 Alice Miranda Ollstein, "'There is no Surge Plan': Despite Warnings, Congress Failed to Fully Fund Pandemics Bill," *Politico*, March 28, 2020, https://www.politico.com/news/2020/03/28/congress-pandemic-bill-coronavirus-152580.

66 Ollstein, "'There is no Surge Plan.'"

67 *Wikipedia*, "Crimson Contagion."

68 David E. Sanger, Eric Lipton, Eileen Sullivan, and Michael Crowley, "Before Virus Outbreak: A Cascade of Warnings Went Unheeded," *New York Times*, March 19, 2020 (updated March 22, 2020).

69 Olga Ivshina, "Coronavirus: Space Crew Return to Very Different Earth, *BBC News*, April 17, 2020, https://www.bbc.com/news/world-europe-52300360.

ABOUT THE AUTHOR

Alla Shapiro was born in Ukraine, USSR, and was a first physician-responder to the Chernobyl nuclear catastrophe. In the wake of the extensive cover-up perpetuated by the Soviet government during and after the Chernobyl nuclear disaster and following years of discrimination as a Jewish citizen of the Soviet Union, Alla and her extended family immigrated to the United States in the late 1980s. She completed a residency in general pediatrics at Georgetown University Hospital, followed by a fellowship in pediatric hematology-oncology at the National Institutes of Health, National Cancer Institute. From 2000 to 2003, Dr. Shapiro was a medical officer at the Division of Hematology Oncology Drug Products at the US Food and Drug Administration (FDA). From 2003 to 2019, Dr. Shapiro worked as a medical officer at the Counterterrorism and Emergency Coordination Staff at the FDA.